CW00853803

THE ATOMIC BOMBINGS OF HIROSHIMA AND NAGASAKI

by The Manhattan Engineer District, June 29, 1946

CONTENTS:

FOREWORD

This report describes the effects of the atomic
bombs which were dropped on the Japanese cities
of Hiroshima and Nagasaki on August 6 and 9,
1945, respectively. It summarizes all the authentic
information that is available on damage to
structures, injuries to personnel, morale effect, etc.,
which can be released at this time without
prejudicing the security of the United States.

This report has been compiled by the Manhattan
Engineer District of the United States Army under
the direction of Major General Leslie R. Groves.
Special acknowledgement to those whose work
contributed largely to this report is made to:

The Special Manhattan Engineer District
Investigating Group, The United States Strategic
Bombing Survey, The British Mission to Japan, and

The Joint Atomic Bomb Investigating Group
(Medical). and particularly to the following
individuals:

Col. Stafford L. Warren, Medical Corps, United
States Army, for his evaluation of medical data,

Capt. Henry L. Barnett, Medical Corps, United
States Army, for his evaluation of medical data,

Dr. R. Serber, for his comments on flash burn,

Dr. Hans Bethe, Cornell University, for his

information of the nature of atomic explosions,

Majors Noland Varley and Walter C. Youngs,
Corps of Engineers, United States Army, for their
evaluation of physical damage to structures,

J. 0. Hirschfelder, J. L. Magee, M. Hull, and S. T.
Cohen, of the Los Alamos Laboratory, for their data
on nuclear explosions,

Lieut. Col. David B. Parker, Corps of Engineers,
United States Army, for editing this report.

INTRODUCTION

Statement by the President of the United States:
"Sixteen hours ago an American airplane dropped
one bomb on Hiroshima, Japan, and destroyed its
usefulness to the enemy. That bomb had more
power than 20,000 tons of T.N.T. It had more than
two thousand times the blast power of the British
Grand Slam, which is the largest bomb ever yet
used in the history of warfare".

These fateful words of the President on August 6th,
1945, marked the first public announcement of the
greatest scientific achievement in history. The
atomic bomb, first tested in New Mexico on July
16, 1945, had just been used against a military
target.

On August 6th, 1945, at 8:15 A.M., Japanese time,
a B-29 heavy bomber flying at high altitude
dropped the first atomic bomb on Hiroshima. More
than 4 square miles of the city were instantly and
completely devastated. 66,000 people were killed,
and 69,000 injured.

On August 9th, three days later, at 11:02 A.M.,
another B-29 dropped the second bomb on the
industrial section of the city of Nagasaki, totally
destroying 1 1/2 square miles of the city, killing
39,000 persons, and injuring 25,000 more.

On August 10, the day after the atomic bombing of
Nagasaki, the Japanese government requested that it
be permitted to surrender under the terms of the
Potsdam declaration of July 26th which it had

previously ignored.

THE MANHATTAN PROJECT ATOMIC BOMB INVESTIGATING GROUP

On August 11th, 1945, two days after the bombing of Nagasaki, a message was dispatched from Major General Leslie R. Groves to Brigadier General Thomas F. Farrell, who was his deputy in atomic bomb work and was representing him in operations in the Pacific, directing him to organize a special Manhattan Project Atomic Bomb Investigating Group.

This Group was to secure scientific, technical and medical intelligence in the atomic bomb field from within Japan as soon as possible after the cessation of hostilities. The mission was to consist of three groups:

1. Group for Hiroshima. 2. Group for Nagasaki. 3. Group to secure information concerning general Japanese activities in the field of atomic bombs.

The first two groups were organized to accompany the first American troops into Hiroshima and Nagasaki.

The primary purposes of the mission were as follows, in order of importance:

1. To make certain that no unusual hazards were present in the bombed cities.

2. To secure all possible information concerning the effects of the bombs, both usual and unusual, and particularly with regard to radioactive effects, if any, on the targets or elsewhere.

General Groves further stated that all available specialist personnel and instruments would be sent from the United States, and that the Supreme Allied Commander in the Pacific would be informed about the organization of the mission.

On the same day, 11 August, the special personnel who formed the part of the investigating group to be sent from the United States were selected and ordered to California with instructions to proceed overseas at once to accomplish the purposes set forth in the message to General Farrell. The main party departed from Hamilton Field, California on the morning of 13 August and arrived in the Marianas on 15 August.

On 12 August the Chief of Staff sent the Theater Commander the following message:

"FOR MACARTHUR, SIGNED MARSHALL:

"GROVES HAS ORDERED FARRELL AT TINIAN TO ORGANIZE A SCIENTIFIC GROUP OF THREE SECTIONS FOR POTENTIAL USE IN JAPAN IF SUCH USE SHOULD BE DESIRED. THE FIRST GROUP IS FOR HIROSHIMA, THE SECOND FOR NAGASAKI, AND THE THIRD FOR THE PURPOSE OF SECURING INFORMATION CONCERNING GENERAL JAPANESE ACTIVITIES IN THE

FIELD OF ATOMIC WEAPONS. THE GROUPS FOR HIROSHIMA AND NAGASAKI SHOULD ENTER THOSE CITIES WITH THE FIRST AMERICAN TROOPS IN ORDER THAT THESE TROOPS SHALL NOT BE SUBJECTED TO ANY POSSIBLE TOXIC EFFECTS ALTHOUGH WE HAVE NO REASON TO BELIEVE THAT ANY SUCH EFFECTS ACTUALLY EXIST. FARRELL AND HIS ORGANIZATION HAVE ALL AVAILABLE INFORMATION ON THIS SUBJECT."

General Farrell arrived in Yokohama on 30 August, with the Commanding General of the 8th Army; Colonel Warren, who was Chief of the Radiological Division of the District, arrived on 7 September. The main body of the investigating group followed later. Preliminary inspections of Hiroshima and Nagasaki were made on 8-9 and 13-14 September, respectively. Members of the press had been enabled to precede General Farrell to Hiroshima.

The special groups spent 16 days in Nagasaki and 4 days in Hiroshima, during which time they collected as much information as was possible under their directives which called for a prompt report. After General Farrell returned to the U.S. to make his preliminary report, the groups were headed by Brigadier General J. B. Newman, Jr. More extensive surveys have been made since that time by other agencies who had more time and personnel available for the purpose, and much of their additional data has thrown further light on the effects of the bombings. This data has been duly considered in the making of this report.

PROPAGANDA

On the day after the Hiroshima strike, General
Farrell received instructions from the War
Department to engage in a propaganda campaign
against the Japanese Empire in connection with the
new weapon and its use against Hiroshima. The
campaign was to include leaflets and any other
propaganda considered appropriate. With the fullest
cooperation from CINCPAC of the Navy and the
United States Strategic Air Forces, he initiated
promptly a campaign which included the
preparation and distribution of leaflets, broadcasting
via short wave every 15 minutes over radio Saipan
and the printing at Saipan and distribution over the
Empire of a Japanese language newspaper which
included the description and photographs of the
Hiroshima strike. *Try and get hold of a copy?*

The campaign proposed:

1. Dropping 16,000,000 leaflets in a period of 9
days on 47 Japanese cities with population of over
100,000. These cities represented more than 40% of
the total population.

2. Broadcast of propaganda at regular intervals over
radio Saipan.

3. Distribution of 500,000 Japanese language
newspapers containing stories and pictures of the
atomic bomb attacks.

The campaign continued until the Japanese began
their surrender negotiations. At that time some

6,000,000 leaflets and a large number of newspapers had been dropped. The radio broadcasts in Japanese had been carried out at regular 15 minute intervals.

SUMMARY OF DAMAGES AND INJURIES

Both the Hiroshima and the Nagasaki atomic bombs exhibited similar effects.

The damages to man-made structures and other inanimate objects was the result in both cities of the following effects of the explosions:

A. Blast, or pressure wave, similar to that of normal explosions.

B. Primary fires, i.e., those fires started instantaneously by the heat radiated from the atomic explosion.

C. Secondary fires, i.e., those fires resulting from the collapse of buildings, damage to electrical systems, overturning of stoves, and other primary effects of the blast.

D. Spread of the original fires (B and C) to other structures.

The casualties sustained by the inhabitants of both cities were due to:

A. "Flash" burns, caused directly by the almost

instantaneous radiation of heat and light at the moment of the explosion.

B. Burns resulting from the fires caused by the explosion.

C. Mechanical injuries caused by collapse of buildings, flying debris, and forceable hurling - about of persons struck by the blast pressure waves.

D. Radiation injuries caused by the instantaneous penetrating radiation (in many respects similar to excessive X-ray exposure) from the nuclear explosion; all of these effective radiations occurred during the first minute after initiation of the explosion, and nearly all occurred during the first second of the explosion.

No casualties were suffered as a result of any persistent radioactivity of fission products of the bomb, or any induced radioactivity of objects near the explosion. The gamma radiations emitted by the nuclear explosion did not, of course, inflict any damage on structures.

The number of casualties which resulted from the pure blast effect alone (i.e., because of simple pressure) was probably negligible in comparison to that caused by other effects.

The central portions of the cities underneath the explosions suffered almost complete destruction. The only surviving objects were the frames of a small number of strong reinforced concrete buildings which were not collapsed by the blast;

most of these buildings suffered extensive damage from interior fires, had their windows, doors, and partitions knocked out, and all other fixtures which were not integral parts of the reinforced concrete frames burned or blown away; the casualties in such buildings near the center of explosion were almost 100%. In Hiroshima fires sprang up simultaneously all over the wide flat central area of the city; these fires soon combined in an immense "fire storm" (high winds blowing inwards toward the center of a large conflagration) similar to those caused by ordinary mass incendiary raids; the resulting terrific conflagration burned out almost everything which had not already been destroyed by the blast in a roughly circular area of 4.4 square miles around the point directly under the explosion (this point will hereafter in this report be referred to as X). Similar fires broke out in Nagasaki, but no devastating fire storm resulted as in Hiroshima because of the irregular shape of the city.

In both cities the blast totally destroyed everything within a radius of 1 mile from the center of explosion, except for certain reinforced concrete frames as noted above. The atomic explosion almost completely destroyed Hiroshima's identity as a city. Over a fourth of the population was killed in one stroke and an additional fourth seriously injured, so that even if there had been no damage to structures and installations the normal city life would still have been completely shattered. Nearly everything was heavily damaged up to a radius of 3 miles from the blast, and beyond this distance damage, although comparatively light, extended for several more miles. Glass was broken up to 12 miles.

In Nagasaki, a smaller area of the city was actually destroyed than in Hiroshima, because the hills which enclosed the target area restricted the spread of the great blast; but careful examination of the effects of the explosion gave evidence of even greater blast effects than in Hiroshima. Total destruction spread over an area of about 3 square miles. Over a third of the 50,000 buildings in the target area of Nagasaki were destroyed or seriously damaged. The complete destruction of the huge steel works and the torpedo plant was especially impressive. The steel frames of all buildings within a mile of the explosion were pushed away, as by a giant hand, from the point of detonation. The badly burned area extended for 3 miles in length. The hillsides up to a radius of 8,000 feet were scorched, giving them an autumnal appearance.

MAIN CONCLUSIONS

The following are the main conclusions which were reached after thorough examination of the effects of the bombs dropped on Hiroshima and Nagasaki:

1. No harmful amounts of persistent radioactivity were present after the explosions as determined by:

A. Measurements of the intensity of radioactivity at the time of the investigation; and

B. Failure to find any clinical evidence of persons harmed by persistent radioactivity.

The effects of the atomic bombs on human beings were of three main types:

A. Burns, remarkable for (1) the great ground area over which they were inflicted and (2) the prevalence of "flash" burns caused by the instantaneous heat radiation.

B. Mechanical injuries, also remarkable for the wide area in which suffered.

C. Effects resulting from penetrating gamma radiation. The effects from radiation were due to instantaneous discharge of radiation at the moment of explosion and not to persistent radioactivity (of either fission products or other substances whose radioactivity might have been induced by proximity to the explosions).

The effects of the atomic bombs on structures and installations were of two types:

A. Destruction caused by the great pressure from the blast; and

B. Destruction caused by the fires, either started directly by the great heat radiation, or indirectly through the collapse of buildings, wiring, etc.

4. The actual tonnage of T.N.T. which would have caused the same blast damage was approximately of the order of 20,000 tons.

5. In respect to their height of burst, the bombs

performed exactly according to design.

6. The bombs were placed in such positions that they could not have done more damage from any alternative bursting point in either city.

7. The heights of burst were correctly chosen having regard to the type of destruction it was desired to cause.

8. The information collected would enable a reasonably accurate prediction to be made of the blast damage likely to be caused in any city where an atomic explosion could be effected.

THE SELECTION OF THE TARGET

Some of the most frequent queries concerning the atomic bombs are those dealing with the selection of the targets and the decision as to when the bombs would be used.

The approximate date for the first use of the bomb was set in the fall of 1942 after the Army had taken over the direction of and responsibility for the atomic bomb project. At that time, under the scientific assumptions which turned out to be correct, the summer of 1945 was named as the most likely date when sufficient production would have been achieved to make it possible actually to construct and utilize an atomic bomb. It was essential before this time to develop the technique of constructing and detonating the bomb and to make an almost infinite number of scientific and engineering developments and tests. Between the fall of 1942 and June 1945, the estimated probabilities of success had risen from about 60% to above 90%; however, not until July 16, 1945, when the first full-scale test took place in New Mexico, was it conclusively proven that the theories, calculations, and engineering were correct and that the bomb would be successful.

photographs?
records. The test in <u>New Mexico</u> was held 6 days after sufficient material had become available for the first bomb. The Hiroshima bomb was ready awaiting suitable weather on July 31st, and the Nagasaki bomb was used as soon after the Hiroshima bomb as it was practicable to operate the second mission.

The work on the actual selection of targets for the atomic bomb was begun in the spring of 1945. This was done in close cooperation with the Commanding General, Army Air Forces, and his Headquarters. A number of experts in various fields assisted in the study. These included mathematicians, theoretical physicists, experts on the blast effects of bombs, weather consultants, and various other specialists. Some of the important considerations were:

A. The range of the aircraft which would carry the bomb.

B. The desirability of visual bombing in order to insure the most effective use of the bomb.

C. Probable weather conditions in the target areas.

D. Importance of having one primary and two secondary targets for each mission, so that if weather conditions prohibited bombing the target there would be at least two alternates.

E. Selection of targets to produce the greatest military effect on the Japanese people and thereby most effectively shorten the war.

F. The morale effect upon the enemy.

These led in turn to the following:

A. Since the atomic bomb was expected to produce its greatest amount of damage by primary blast effect, and next greatest by fires, the targets should contain a large percentage of closely-built frame buildings and other construction that would be most susceptible to damage by blast and fire.

B. The maximum blast effect of the bomb was calculated to extend over an area of approximately 1 mile in radius; therefore the selected targets should contain a densely built-up area of at least this size.

C. The selected targets should have a high military strategic value.

D. The first target should be relatively untouched by previous bombing, in order that the effect of a single atomic bomb could be determined.

The weather records showed that for five years

there had never been two successive good visual bombing days over Tokyo, indicating what might be expected over other targets in the home islands. The worst month of the year for visual bombing was believed to be June, after which the weather should improve slightly during July and August and then become worse again during September. Since good bombing conditions would occur rarely, the most intense plans and preparations were necessary in order to secure accurate weather forecasts and to arrange for full utilization of whatever good weather might occur. It was also very desirable to start the raids before September.

DESCRIPTION OF THE CITIES BEFORE THE BOMBINGS

Hiroshima

The city of Hiroshima is located on the broad, flat delta of the Ota River, which has 7 channel outlets dividing the city into six islands which project into Hiroshima Bay. The city is almost entirely flat and only slightly above sea level; to the northwest and northeast of the city some hills rise to 700 feet. A single hill in the eastern part of the city proper about 1/2 mile long and 221 feet in height interrupted to some extent the spreading of the blast damage; otherwise the city was fully exposed to the bomb. Of a city area of over 26 square miles, only 7 square miles were completely built-up. There was no marked separation of commercial, industrial, and residential zones. 75% of the population was concentrated in the densely built-up area in the center of the city.

Hiroshima was a city of considerable military importance. It contained the 2nd Army Headquarters, which commanded the defense of all of southern Japan. The city was a communications center, a storage point, and an assembly area for troops. To quote a Japanese report, "Probably more than a thousand times since the beginning of the war did the Hiroshima citizens see off with cries of 'Banzai' the troops leaving from the harbor."

The center of the city contained a number of reinforced concrete buildings as well as lighter structures. Outside the center, the area was congested by a dense collection of small wooden workshops set among Japanese houses; a few larger industrial plants lay near the outskirts of the city. The houses were of wooden construction with tile roofs. Many of the industrial buildings also were of wood frame construction. The city as a whole was highly susceptible to fire damage.

Some of the reinforced concrete buildings were of a far stronger construction than is required by normal standards in America, because of the earthquake danger in Japan. This exceptionally strong construction undoubtedly accounted for the fact that the framework of some of the buildings which were fairly close to the center of damage in the city did not collapse.

The population of Hiroshima had reached a peak of over 380,000 earlier in the war but prior to the

atomic bombing the population had steadily decreased because of a systematic evacuation ordered by the Japanese government. At the time of the attack the population was approximately 255,000. This figure is based on the registered population, used by the Japanese in computing ration quantities, and the estimates of additional workers and troops who were brought into the city may not be highly accurate. Hiroshima thus had approximately the same number of people as the city of Providence, R.I., or Dallas, Tex.

Nagasaki

Nagasaki lies at the head of a long bay which forms the best natural harbor on the southern Japanese home island of Kyushu. The main commercial and residential area of the city lies on a small plain near the end of the bay. Two rivers divided by a mountain spur form the two main valleys in which the city lies. This mountain spur and the irregular lay-out of the city tremendously reduced the area of destruction, so that at first glance Nagasaki appeared to have been less devastated than Hiroshima.

The heavily build-up area of the city is confined by the terrain to less than 4 square miles out of a total of about 35 square miles in the city as a whole.

The city of Nagasaki had been one of the largest sea ports in southern Japan and was of great war-time importance because of its many and varied industries, including the production of ordnance, ships, military equipment, and other war materials.

The narrow long strip attacked was of particular importance because of its industries.

In contrast to many modern aspects of Nagasaki, the residences almost without exception were of flimsy, typical Japanese construction, consisting of wood or wood-frame buildings, with wood walls with or without plaster, and tile roofs. Many of the smaller industries and business establishments were also housed in wooden buildings or flimsily built masonry buildings. Nagasaki had been permitted to grow for many years without conforming to any definite city zoning plan and therefore residences were constructed adjacent to factory buildings and to each other almost as close as it was possible to build them throughout the entire industrial valley.

THE ATTACKS

Hiroshima

Hiroshima was the primary target of the first atomic bomb mission. The mission went smoothly in every respect. The weather was good, and the crew and equipment functioned perfectly. In every detail, the attack was carried out exactly as planned, and the bomb performed exactly as expected. *aware of potential devastation.*

The bomb exploded over Hiroshima at 8:15 on the morning of August 6, 1945. About an hour previously, the Japanese early warning radar net had detected the approach of some American aircraft headed for the southern part of Japan. The alert had been given and radio broadcasting stopped in many cities, among them Hiroshima. The planes approached the coast at a very high altitude. At nearly 8:00 A.M., the radar operator in Hiroshima determined that the number of planes coming in was very small - probably not more than three - and the air raid alert was lifted. The normal radio broadcast warning was given to the people that it might be advisable to go to shelter if B-29's were actually sighted, but no raid was expected beyond some sort of reconnaissance. At 8:15 A.M., the bomb exploded with a blinding flash in the sky, and a great rush of air and a loud rumble of noise extended for many miles around the city; the first blast was soon followed by the sounds of falling buildings and of growing fires, and a great cloud of dust and smoke began to cast a pall of darkness over the city.

At 8:16 A.M., the Tokyo control operator of the Japanese Broadcasting Corporation noticed that the Hiroshima station had gone off the air. He tried to use another telephone line to reestablish his program, but it too had failed. About twenty minutes later the Tokyo railroad telegraph center realized that the main line telegraph had stopped working just north of Hiroshima. From some small railway stops within ten miles of the city there came unofficial and confused reports of a terrible explosion in Hiroshima. All these reports were transmitted to the Headquarters of the Japanese General Staff.

Military headquarters repeatedly tried to call the Army Control Station in Hiroshima. The complete silence from that city puzzled the men at Headquarters; they knew that no large enemy raid could have occurred, and they knew that no sizeable store of explosives was in Hiroshima at that time. A young officer of the Japanese General Staff was instructed to fly immediately to Hiroshima, to land, survey the damage, and return to Tokyo with reliable information for the staff. It was generally felt at Headquarters that nothing serious had taken place, that it was all a terrible rumor starting from a few sparks of truth.

The staff officer went to the airport and took off for the southwest. After flying for about three hours, while still nearly 100 miles from Hiroshima, he and his pilot saw a great cloud of smoke from the bomb. In the bright afternoon, the remains of Hiroshima were burning.

Their plane soon reached the city, around which they circled in disbelief. A great scar on the land, still burning, and covered by a heavy cloud of smoke, was all that was left of a great city. They landed south of the city, and the staff officer immediately began to organize relief measures, after reporting to Tokyo.

only leant of devastation here.

Tokyo's first knowledge of what had really caused the disaster came from the White House public announcement in Washington sixteen hours after Hiroshima had been hit by the atomic bomb.

Nagasaki

Nagasaki had never been subjected to large scale

bombing prior to the explosion of the atomic bomb there. On August 1st, 1945, however, a number of high explosive bombs were dropped on the city. A few of these bombs hit in the shipyards and dock areas in the southwest portion of the city. Several of the bombs hit the Mitsubishi Steel and Arms Works and six bombs landed at the Nagasaki Medical School and Hospital, with three direct hits on buildings there. While the damage from these few bombs were relatively small, it created considerable concern in Nagasaki and a number of people, principally school children, were evacuated to rural areas for safety, thus reducing the population in the city at the time of the atomic attack.

On the morning of August 9th, 1945, at about 7:50 A.M., Japanese time, an air raid alert was sounded in Nagasaki, but the "All clear" signal was given at 8:30. When only two B-29 superfortresses were sighted at 10:53 the Japanese apparently assumed that the planes were only on reconnaissance and no further alarm was given. A few moments later, at 11:00 o'clock, the observation B-29 dropped instruments attached to three parachutes and at 11:02 the other plane released the atomic bomb.

The bomb exploded high over the industrial valley of Nagasaki, almost midway between the Mitsubishi Steel and Arms Works, in the south, and the Mitsubishi-Urakami Ordnance Works (Torpedo Works), in the north, the two principal targets of the city.

Despite its extreme importance, the first bombing mission on Hiroshima had been almost routine. The second mission was not so uneventful. Again the crew was specially trained and selected; but bad weather introduced some momentous complications. These complications are best described in the brief account of the mission's weaponeer, Comdr., now Capt., F. L. Ashworth, U.S.N., who was in technical command of the bomb and was charged with the responsibility of insuring that the bomb was successfully dropped at the proper time and on the designated target. His narrative runs as follows:

"The night of our take-off was one of tropical rain squalls, and flashes of lightning stabbed into the darkness with disconcerting regularity. The weather forecast told us of storms all the way from the Marianas to the Empire. Our rendezvous was to be off the southeast coast of Kyushu, some 1500 miles away. There we were to join with our two companion observation B-29's that took off a few minutes behind us. Skillful piloting and expert navigation brought us to the rendezvous without incident.

"About five minutes after our arrival, we were joined by the first of our B-29's. The second, however, failed to arrive, having apparently been thrown off its course by storms during the night. We waited 30 minutes and then proceeded without the second plane toward the target area.

"During the approach to the target the special instruments installed in the plane told us that the bomb was ready to function. We were prepared to drop the second atomic bomb on Japan. But fate was against us, for the target was completely obscured by smoke and haze. Three times we attempted bombing runs, but without success. Then with anti-aircraft fire bursting around us and with a number of enemy fighters coming up after us, we headed for our secondary target, Nagasaki.

"The bomb burst with a blinding flash and a huge column of black smoke swirled up toward us. Out of this column of smoke there boiled a great swirling mushroom of gray smoke, luminous with red, flashing flame, that reached to 40,000 feet in less than 8 minutes. Below through the clouds we could see the pall of black smoke ringed with fire that covered what had been the industrial area of Nagasaki.

"By this time our fuel supply was dangerously low, so after one quick circle of Nagasaki, we headed direct for Okinawa for an emergency landing and refueling".

GENERAL COMPARISON OF HIROSHIMA AND NAGASAKI

It was not at first apparent to even trained observers visiting the two Japanese cities which of the two bombs had been the most effective.

In some respects, Hiroshima looked worse than Nagasaki. The fire damage in Hiroshima was much more complete; the center of the city was hit and everything but the reinforced concrete buildings had virtually disappeared. A desert of clear-swept, charred remains, with only a few strong building frames left standing was a terrifying sight.

At Nagasaki there were no buildings just underneath the center of explosion. The damage to the Mitsubishi Arms Works and the Torpedo Works was spectacular, but not overwhelming. There was something left to see, and the main contours of some of the buildings were still normal.

An observer could stand in the center of Hiroshima and get a view of the most of the city; the hills prevented a similar overall view in Nagasaki. Hiroshima impressed itself on one's mind as a vast expanse of desolation; but nothing as vivid was left in one's memory of Nagasaki.

When the observers began to note details, however, striking differences appeared. Trees were down in both cities, but the large trees which fell in Hiroshima were uprooted, while those in Nagasaki were actually snapped off. A few reinforced concrete buildings were smashed at the center in Hiroshima, but in Nagasaki equally heavy damage could be found 2,300 feet from X. In the study of objects which gave definite clues to the blast pressure, such as squashed tin cans, dished metal plates, bent or snapped poles and like, it was soon evident that the Nagasaki bomb had been much more effective than the Hiroshima bomb. In the description of damage which follows, it will be noted that the radius for the amount of damage was greater in Nagasaki than Hiroshima.

GENERAL DESCRIPTION OF DAMAGE CAUSED BY THE ATOMIC EXPLOSIONS

In considering the devastation in the two cities, it should be remembered that the cities' differences in shape and topography resulted in great differences in the damages. Hiroshima was all on low, flat ground, and was roughly circular in shape; Nagasaki was much cut up by hills and mountain spurs, with no regularity to its shape.

In Hiroshima almost everything up to about one mile from X was completely destroyed, except for a small number (about 50) of heavily reinforced concrete buildings, most of which were specially designed to withstand earthquake shock, which were not collapsed by the blast; most of these buildings had their interiors completely gutted, and all windows, doors, sashes, and frames ripped out. In Nagasaki, nearly everything within 1/2 mile of the explosion was destroyed, including heavy structures. All Japanese homes were destroyed within 1 1/2 miles from X.

Underground air raid shelters with earth cover roofs immediately below the explosion had their roofs caved in; but beyond 1/2 mile from X they suffered no damage.

In Nagasaki, 1500 feet from X high quality steel frame buildings were not completely collapsed, but the entire buildings suffered mass distortion and all panels and roofs were blown in.

In Nagasaki, 2,000 feet from X, reinforced concrete buildings with 10" walls and 6" floors were collapsed; reinforced concrete buildings with 4" walls and roofs were standing but were badly damaged. At 2,000 feet some 9" concrete walls were completely destroyed.

In Nagasaki, 3,500 feet from X, church buildings with 18" brick walls were completely destroyed. 12" brick walls were severely cracked as far as 5,000 feet.

In Hiroshima, 4,400 feet from X, multi-story brick buildings were completely demolished. In Nagasaki, similar buildings were destroyed to 5,300 feet.

In Hiroshima, roof tiles were bubbled (melted) by the flash heat out to 4,000 feet from X; in Nagasaki, the same effect was observed to 6,500 feet.

In Hiroshima, steel frame buildings were destroyed 4,200 feet from X, and to 4,800 feet in Nagasaki.

In both cities, the mass distortion of large steel buildings was observed out to 4,500 feet from X.

In Nagasaki, reinforced concrete smoke stacks with 8" walls, specially designed to withstand earthquake shocks, were overturned up to 4,000 feet from X.

In Hiroshima, steel frame buildings suffered severe structural damage up to 5,700 feet from X, and in Nagasaki the same damage was sustained as far as 6,000 feet.

In Nagasaki, 9" brick walls were heavily cracked to 5,000 feet, were moderately cracked to 6,000 feet, and slightly cracked to 8,000 feet. In both cities, light concrete buildings collapsed out to 4,700 feet.

In Hiroshima, multi-story brick buildings suffered structural damage up to 6,600 feet, and in Nagasaki up to 6,500 feet from X.

In both cities overhead electric installations were destroyed up to 5,500 feet; and trolley cars were destroyed up to 5,500 feet, and damaged to 10,500 feet.

Flash ignition of dry, combustible material was observed as far as 6,400 feet from X in Hiroshima, and in Nagasaki as far as 10,000 feet from X.

Severe damage to gas holders occured out to 6,500 feet in both cities.

All Japanese homes were seriously damaged up to 6,500 feet in Hiroshima, and to 8,000 feet in Nagasaki. Most Japanese homes were damaged up to 8,000 feet in Hiroshima and 10,500 feet in Nagasaki.

The hillsides in Nagasaki were scorched by the flash radiation of heat as far as 8,000 feet from X; this scorching gave the hillsides the appearance of premature autumn.

In Nagasaki, very heavy plaster damage was observed in many buildings up to 9,000 feet; moderate damage was sustained as far as 12,000 feet, and light damage up to 15,000 feet.

The flash charring of wooden telegraph poles was observed up to 9,500 feet from X in Hiroshima, and to 11,000 feet in Nagasaki; some reports indicate flash burns as far as 13,000 feet from X in both places.

Severe displacement of roof tiles was observed up to 8,000 feet in Hiroshima, and to 10,000 feet in Nagasaki.

In Nagasaki, very heavy damage to window frames and doors was observed up to 8,000 feet, and light damage up to 12,000 feet.

Roofs and wall coverings on steel frame buildings were destroyed out to 11,000 feet.

Although the sources of many fires were difficult to trace accurately, it is believed that fires were started by primary heat radiation as far as 15,000 feet from X.

Roof damage extended as far as 16,000 feet from X in Hiroshima and in Nagasaki.

The actual collapse of buildings was observed at the extreme range of 23,000 feet from X in Nagasaki.

Although complete window damage was observed only up to 12,000 feet from X, some window damage occurred in Nagasaki up to 40,000 feet, and actual breakage of glass occured up to 60,000 feet.

Heavy fire damage was sustained in a circular area in Hiroshima with a mean radius of about 6,000 feet and a maximum radius of about 11,000 feet; similar heavy damage occured in Nagasaki south of X up to 10,000 feet, where it was stopped on a river course.

In Hiroshima over 60,000 of 90,000 buildings were destroyed or severely damaged by the atomic bomb; this figure represents over 67% of the city's structures.

In Nagasaki 14,000 or 27% of 52,000 residences were completely destroyed and 5,40O, or 10% were half destroyed. Only 12% remained undamaged. This destruction was limited by the layout of the city. The following is a summary of the damage to buildings in Nagasaki as determined from a ground survey made by the Japanese:

Destruction of Buildings and Houses Number Percentage (Compiled by Nagasaki Municipality)

Total in Nagasaki (before atomic explosion) 50,000 100.0 Blasted (not burned) 2,652 5.3 Blasted and burned 11,494 23.0 Blasted and/or burned 14,146 28.3 Partially burned or blasted 5,441 10.9 Total buildings and houses destroyed 19,587 39.2 Undamaged 30,413 60.8

In Hiroshima, all utilities and transportation services were disrupted for varying lengths of time. In general however services were restored about as rapidly as they could be used by the depleted population. Through railroad service was in order in Hiroshima on 8 August, and electric power was available in most of the surviving parts on 7 August, the day after the bombing. The reservoir of the city was not damaged, being nearly 2 miles from X. However, 70,000 breaks in water pipes in buildings and dwellings were caused by the blast and fire effects. Rolling transportation suffered extensive damage. The damage to railroad tracks, and roads was comparatively small, however. The electric power transmission and distribution systems were badly wrecked. The telephone system was approximately 80% damaged, and no service was restored until 15 August.

Despite the customary Japanese lack of attention to sanitation measures, no major epidemic broke out in the bombed cities. Although the conditions following the bombings makes this fact seem surprising, the experience of other bombed cities in both Germany and Japan show Hiroshima and Nagasaki not to be isolated cases.

The atomic explosion over Nagasaki affected an over-all area of approximately 42.9 square miles of which about 8.5 square miles were water and only about 9.8 square miles were built up, the remainder being partially settled. Approximately 36% of the built up areas were seriously damaged. The area most severely damaged had an average radius of about 1 mile, and covered about 2.9 square miles of which 2.4 were built up.

In Nagasaki, buildings with structural steel frames, principally the Mitsubishi Plant as far as 6,000 feet from X were severely damaged; these buildings were typical of wartime mill construction in

America and Great Britain, except that some of the
frames were somewhat less substantial. The damage
consisted of windows broken out (100%), steel
sashes ripped out or bent, corrugated metal or
corrugated asbestos roofs and sidings ripped off,
roofs bent or destroyed, roof trusses collapsed,
columns bent and cracked and concrete foundations
for columns rotated. Damage to buildings with
structural steel frames was more severe where the
buildings received the effect of the blast on their
sides than where the blast hit the ends of buildings,
because the buildings had more stiffness (resistance
to negative moment at the top of columns) in a
longitudinal direction. Many of the lightly
constructed steel frame buildings collapsed
completely while some of the heavily constructed
(to carry the weight of heavy cranes and loads) were
stripped of roof and siding, but the frames were
only partially injured.

The next most seriously damaged area in Nagasaki
lies outside the 2.9 square miles just described, and
embraces approximately 4.2 square miles of which
29% was built up. The damage from blast and fire
was moderate here, but in some sections (portions
of main business districts) many secondary fires
started and spread rapidly, resulting in about as
much over-all destruction as in areas much closer to
X.

An area of partial damage by blast and fire lies just
outside the one just described and comprises
approximately 35.8 square miles. Of this area,
roughly 1/6th was built up and 1/4th was water. The
extent of damage varied from serious (severe

damage to roofs and windows in the main business section of Nagasaki, 2.5 miles from X), to minor (broken or occasionally broken windows at a distance of 7 miles southeast of X).

As intended, the bomb was exploded at an almost ideal location over Nagasaki to do the maximum damage to industry, including the Mitsubishi Steel and Arms Works, the Mitsubishi-Urakami Ordnance Works (Torpedo Works), and numerous factories, factory training schools, and other industrial establishments, with a minimum destruction of dwellings and consequently, a minimum amount of casualties. Had the bomb been dropped farther south, the Mitsubishi-Urakami Ordnance Works would not have been so severely damaged, but the main business and residential districts of Nagasaki would have sustained much greater damage casualties.

Calculations show that the structural steel and reinforced concrete frames which survived the blast fairly close to X could not have withstood the estimated peak pressures developed against the total areas presented by the sides and roof of the buildings. The survival of these frames is explained by the fact that they were not actually required to withstand the peak pressure because the windows were quickly knocked out and roof and siding stripped off thereby reducing total area and relieving the pressure. While this saved the building frame, it permitted severe damage to building interior and contents, and injuries to the building occupants. Buildings without large panel openings through which the pressure could dissipate were completely crushed, even when their frames were as strong as those which survived.

The damage sustained by reinforced concrete buildings depended both on the proximity to X and the type and strength of the reinforced concrete construction. Some of the buildings with reinforced concrete frames also had reinforced concrete walls, ceilings, and partitions, while others had brick or concrete tile walls covered either with plaster or ornamental stone, with partitions of metal, glass, and plaster. With the exception of the Nagasaki Medical School and Hospital group, which was designed to withstand earthquakes and was therefore of heavier construction than most American structures, most of the reinforced concrete structures could be classified only as fair, with concrete of low strength and density, with many of the columns, beams, and slabs underdesigned and improperly reinforced. These facts account for some of the structural failures which occured.

In general, the atomic bomb explosion damaged all windows and ripped out, bent, or twisted most of the steel window or door sashes, ripped doors from hinges, damaged all suspended wood, metal, and plaster ceilings. The blast concussion also caused great damage to equipment by tumbling and battering. Fires generally of secondary origin consumed practically all combustible material, caused plaster to crack off, burned all wooden trim, stair covering, wooden frames of wooden suspended ceilings, beds, mattresses, and mats, and fused glass, ruined all equipment not already destroyed by the blast, ruined all electrical wiring, plumbing, and caused spalling of concrete columns and beams in many of the rooms.

Almost without exception masonry buildings of either brick or stone within the effective limits of the blast were severely damaged so that most of them were flattened or reduced to rubble. The wreckage of a church, approximately 1,800 feet east of X in Nagasaki, was one of the few masonry buildings still recognizable and only portions of the walls of this structure were left standing. These walls were extremely thick (about 2 feet). The two domes of the church had reinforced concrete frames and although they were toppled, they held together as units.

Practically every wooden building or building with timber frame within 2.0 miles of X was either completely destroyed or very seriously damaged, and significant damage in Nagasaki resulted as far as 3 miles from X. Nearly all such buildings collapsed and a very large number were consumed by fire.

A reference to the various photographs depicting damage shows that although most of the buildings within the effective limits of the blast were totally destroyed or severely damaged, a large number of chimneys even close to X were left standing, apparently uninjured by the concussion. One explanation is that concrete chimneys are approximately cylindrical in shape and consequently offer much less wind resistance than flat surfaces such as buildings. Another explanation is that since the cities were subject to typhoons the more modern chimneys were probably designed to withstand winds of high velocity. It is also probable that most of the recently constructed chimneys as well as the more modern buildings were constructed to withstand the acceleration of rather severe earthquakes. Since the bombs were exploded high in the air, chimneys relatively close to X were subjected to more of a downward than a lateral pressure, and consequently the overturning moment was much less than might have been anticipated.

Although the blast damaged many bridges to some extent, bridge damage was on the whole slight in comparison to that suffered by buildings. The damage varied from only damaged railings to complete destruction of the superstructure. Some of the bridges were wrecked and the spans were shoved off their piers and into the river bed below by the force of the blast. Others, particularly steel plate girder bridges, were badly buckled by the blast pressure. None of the failures observed could be attributed to inadequate design or structural weaknesses.

The roads, and railroad and street railway trackage sustained practically no primary damage as a result of the explosion. Most of the damage to railroads occurred from secondary causes, such as fires and damage to bridges or other structures. Rolling stock, as well as automobiles, trolleys, and buses were destroyed and burned up to a considerable distance from X. Streets were impassable for awhile because of the debris, but they were not damaged. The height of the bomb explosion probably explains the absence of direct damage to railroads and roads.

A large part of the electric supply was interrupted by the bomb blast chiefly through damage to electric substations and overhead transmission systems. Both gas works in Nagasaki were severely damaged by the bomb. These works would have required 6-7 months to get into operation. In addition to the damage sustained by the electrical and gas systems, severe damage to the water supply system was reported by the Japanese government; the chief damage was a number of breaks in the large water mains and in almost all of the distributing pipes in the areas which were affected by the blast. Nagasaki was still suffering from a water shortage inside the city six weeks after the atomic attack.

The Nagasaki Prefectural report describes vividly the effects of the bomb on the city and its inhabitants:

"Within a radius of 1 kilometer from X, men and animals died almost instantaneously and outside a radius of 1 kilometer and within a radius of 2 kilometers from X, some men and animals died instantly from the great blast and heat but the great majority were seriously or superficially injured. Houses and other structures were completely destroyed while fires broke out everywhere. Trees were uprooted and withered by the heat.

"Outside a radius of 2 kilometers and within a radius of 4 kilometers from X, men and animals suffered various degrees of injury from window glass and other fragments scattered about by the blast and many were burned by the intense heat. Dwellings and other structures were half damaged by blast.

"Outside a radius of 4 kilometers and within a radius of 8 kilometers living creatures were injured by materials blown about by the blast; the majority were only superficially wounded. Houses were only half or partially damaged."

The British Mission to Japan interpreted their observations of the destruction of buildings to apply to similar construction of their own as follows:

A similar bomb exploding in a similar fashion would produce the following effects on normal British houses:

Up to 1,000 yards from X it would cause complete collapse.

Up to 1 mile from X it would damage the houses beyond repair.

Up to 1.5 miles from X it would render them uninhabitable without extensive repair, particularly to roof timbers.

Up to 2.5 miles from X it would render them uninhabitable until first-aid repairs had been carried out.

The fire damage in both cities was tremendous, but

was more complete in Hiroshima than in Nagasaki. The effect of the fires was to change profoundly the appearance of the city and to leave the central part bare, except for some reinforced concrete and steel frames and objects such as safes, chimney stacks, and pieces of twisted sheet metal. The fire damage resulted more from the properties of the cities themselves than from those of the bombs.

The conflagration in Hiroshima caused high winds to spring up as air was drawn in toward the center of the burning area, creating a "fire storm". The wind velocity in the city had been less than 5 miles per hour before the bombing, but the fire-wind attained a velocity of 30-40 miles per hour. These great winds restricted the perimeter of the fire but greatly added to the damage of the conflagration within the perimeter and caused the deaths of many persons who might otherwise have escaped. In Nagasaki, very severe damage was caused by fires, but no extensive "fire storm" engulfed the city. In both cities, some of the fires close to X were no doubt started by the ignition of highly combustible material such as paper, straw, and dry cloth, upon the instantaneous radiation of heat from the nuclear explosion. The presence of large amounts of unburnt combustible materials near X, however, indicated that even though the heat of the blast was very intense, its duration was insufficient to raise the temperature of many materials to the kindling point except in cases where conditions were ideal. The majority of the fires were of secondary origin starting from the usual electrical short-circuits, broken gas lines, overturned stoves, open fires, charcoal braziers, lamps, etc., following collapse or serious damage from the direct blast.

Fire fighting and rescue units were stripped of men and equipment. Almost 30 hours elapsed before any rescue parties were observable. In Hiroshima only a handful of fire engines were available for fighting the ensuing fires, and none of these were of first class type. In any case, however, it is not likely that any fire fighting equipment or personnel or organization could have effected any significant reduction in the amount of damage caused by the tremendous conflagration.

A study of numerous aerial photographs made prior to the atomic bombings indicates that between 10 June and 9 August 1945 the Japanese constructed fire breaks in certain areas of the cities in order to control large scale fires. In general these fire breaks were not effective because fires were started at so many locations simultaneously. They appear, however, to have helped prevent fires from spreading farther east into the main business and residential section of Nagasaki.

TOTAL CASUALTIES

There has been great difficulty in estimating the total casualties in the Japanese cities as a result of the atomic bombing. The extensive destruction of civil installations (hospitals, fire and police department, and government agencies) the state of utter confusion immediately following the explosion, as well as the uncertainty regarding the actual population before the bombing, contribute to the difficulty of making estimates of casualties. The Japanese periodic censuses are not complete. Finally, the great fires that raged in each city totally consumed many bodies.

The number of total casualties has been estimated at various times since the bombings with wide discrepancies. The Manhattan Engineer District's best available figures are:

TABLE A Estimates of Casualties

	Hiroshima	Nagasaki
Pre-raid population	255,000	195,000
Dead	66,000	39,000
Injured	69,000	25,000
Total Casualties	135,000	64,000

The relation of total casualties to distance from X, the center of damage and point directly under the air-burst explosion of the bomb, is of great importance in evaluating the casualty-producing effect of the bombs. This relationship for the total population of Nagasaki is shown in the table below, based on the first-obtained casualty figures of the District:

TABLE B Relation of Total Casualties to Distance from X

Distance from X, feet	Killed	Injured	Missing	Total Casualties	Killed per square mile
0 - 1,640	7,505	960	1,127	9,592	24,700
1,640 - 3,300	3,688	1,478	1,799	6,965	4,040
3,300 - 4,900	8,678	17,137	3,597	29,412	5,710
4,900 - 6,550	221	11,958	28	12,207	125
6,550 - 9,850	112	9,460	17	9,589	20

No figure for total pre-raid population at these different distances were available. Such figures would be necessary in order to compute per cent mortality. A calculation made by the British Mission to Japan and based on a preliminary analysis of the study of the Joint Medical-Atomic Bomb Investigating Commission gives the following calculated values for per cent mortality at increasing distances from X:

TABLE C Per-Cent Mortality at Various Distances

Distance from X, Per-cent Mortality in feet 0 - 1000 93.0% 1000 - 2000 92.0 2000 - 3000 86.0 3000 - 4000 69.0 4000 - 5000 49.0 5000 - 6000 31.5 6000 - 7000 12.5 7000 - 8000 1.3 8000 - 9000 0.5 9000 - 10,000 0.0

It seems almost certain from the various reports that the greatest total number of deaths were those occurring immediately after the bombing. The causes of many of the deaths can only be surmised, and of course many persons near the center of explosion suffered fatal injuries from more than one of the bomb effects. The proper order of importance for possible causes of death is: burns, mechanical injury, and gamma radiation. Early estimates by the Japanese are shown in D below:

TABLE D Cause of Immediate Deaths

City Cause of Death Per-cent of Total Hiroshima Burns 60% Falling debris 30 Other 10

Nagasaki Burns 95% Falling debris 9 Flying glass 7

Other 7

THE NATURE OF AN ATOMIC EXPLOSION

The most striking difference between the explosion of an atomic bomb and that of an ordinary T.N.T. bomb is of course in magnitude; as the President announced after the Hiroshima attack, the explosive energy of each of the atomic bombs was equivalent to about 20,000 tons of T.N.T.

But in addition to its vastly greater power, an atomic explosion has several other very special characteristics. Ordinary explosion is a chemical reaction in which energy is released by the rearrangement of the atoms of the explosive material. In an atomic explosion the identity of the atoms, not simply their arrangement, is changed. A considerable fraction of the mass of the explosive charge, which may be uranium 235 or plutonium, is transformed into energy. Einstein's equation, $E = mc^2$, shows that matter that is transformed into energy may yield a total energy equivalent to the mass multiplied by the square of the velocity of light. The significance of the equation is easily seen when one recalls that the velocity of light is 186,000 miles per second. The energy released when a pound of T.N.T. explodes would, if converted entirely into heat, raise the temperature of 36 lbs. of water from freezing temperature (32 deg F) to boiling temperature (212 deg F). The nuclear fission of a pound of uranium would produce an equal temperature rise in over 200 million pounds of water.

The explosive effect of an ordinary material such as T.N.T. is derived from the rapid conversion of solid T.N.T. to gas, which occupies initially the same volume as the solid; it exerts intense pressures on the surrounding air and expands rapidly to a volume many times larger than the initial volume. A wave of high pressure thus rapidly moves outward from the center of the explosion and is the major cause of damage from ordinary high explosives. An atomic bomb also generates a wave of high pressure which is in fact of, much higher pressure than that from ordinary explosions; and this wave is again the major cause of damage to buildings and other structures. It differs from the pressure wave of a block buster in the size of the area over which high pressures are generated. It also differs in the duration of the pressure pulse at any given point: the pressure from a blockbuster lasts for a few milliseconds (a millisecond is one thousandth of a second) only, that from the atomic bomb for nearly a second, and was felt by observers both in Japan and in New Mexico as a very strong wind going by.

The next greatest difference between the atomic bomb and the T.N.T. explosion is the fact that the atomic bomb gives off greater amounts of radiation. Most of this radiation is "light" of some wave-length ranging from the so-called heat radiations of very long wave length to the so-called gamma rays which have wave-lengths even shorter than the X-rays used in medicine. All of these radiations travel at the same speed; this, the speed of light, is 186,000 miles per second. The radiations are intense enough to kill people within an appreciable distance from the explosion, and are in fact the major cause of deaths and injuries apart from mechanical injuries. The greatest number of radiation injuries was probably due to the ultra-violet rays which have a wave length slightly shorter than visible light and which caused flash burn comparable to severe sunburn. After these, the gamma rays of ultra short wave length are most important; these cause injuries similar to those from over-doses of X-rays.

The origin of the gamma rays is different from that of the bulk of the radiation: the latter is caused by the extremely high temperatures in the bomb, in the same way as light is emitted from the hot surface of the sun or from the wires in an incandescent lamp. The gamma rays on the other hand are emitted by the atomic nuclei themselves when they are transformed in the fission process. The gamma rays are therefore specific to the atomic bomb and are completely absent in T.N.T. explosions. The light of longer wave length (visible and ultra-violet) is also emitted by a T.N.T. explosion, but with much smaller intensity than by an atomic bomb, which makes it insignificant as far as damage is concerned.

A large fraction of the gamma rays is emitted in the first few microseconds (millionths of a second) of the atomic explosion, together with neutrons which are also produced in the nuclear fission. The neutrons have much less damage effect than the gamma rays because they have a smaller intensity and also because they are strongly absorbed in air and therefore can penetrate only to relatively small distances from the explosion: at a thousand yards the neutron intensity is negligible. After the nuclear emission, strong gamma radiation continues to come from the exploded bomb. This generates from the fission products and continues for about one minute until all of the explosion products have risen to such a height that the intensity received on the ground is negligible. A large number of beta rays are also emitted during this time, but they are unimportant because their range is not very great, only a few feet. The range of alpha particles from the unused active material and fissionable material of the bomb is even smaller.

Apart from the gamma radiation ordinary light is emitted, some of which is visible and some of which is the ultra violet rays mainly responsible for flash burns. The emission of light starts a few milliseconds after the nuclear explosion when the energy from the explosion reaches the air surrounding the bomb. The observer sees then a ball of fire which rapidly grows in size. During most of the early time, the ball of fire extends as far as the wave of high pressure. As the ball of fire grows its temperature and brightness decrease. Several milliseconds after the initiation of the explosion, the brightness of the ball of fire goes through a minimum, then it gets somewhat brighter and remains at the order of a few times the brightness of the sun for a period of 10 to 15 seconds for an observer at six miles distance. Most of the radiation is given off after this point of maximum brightness. Also after this maximum, the pressure waves run ahead of the ball of fire.

The ball of fire rapidly expands from the size of the bomb to a radius of several hundred feet at one second after the explosion. After this the most striking feature is the rise of the ball of fire at the rate of about 30 yards per second. Meanwhile it also continues to expand by mixing with the cooler air surrounding it. At the end of the first minute the ball has expanded to a radius of several hundred yards and risen to a height of about one mile. The shock wave has by now reached a radius of 15 miles and its pressure dropped to less than 1/10 of a pound per square inch. The ball now loses its brilliance and appears as a great cloud of smoke: the pulverized material of the bomb. This cloud continues to rise vertically and finally mushrooms out at an altitude of about 25,000 feet depending upon meteorological conditions. The cloud reaches a maximum height of between 50,000 and 70,000 feet in a time of over 30 minutes.

It is of interest to note that Dr. Hans Bethe, then a member of the Manhattan Engineer District on loan from Cornell University, predicted the existence and characteristics of this ball of fire months before the first test was carried out.

To summarize, radiation comes in two bursts - an extremely intense one lasting only about 3 milliseconds and a less intense one of much longer duration lasting several seconds. The second burst contains by far the larger fraction of the total light energy, more than 90%. But the first flash is especially large in ultra-violet radiation which is biologically more effective. Moreover, because the heat in this flash comes in such a short time, there is no time for any cooling to take place, and the temperature of a person's skin can be raised 50 degrees centigrade by the flash of visible and ultra-violet rays in the first millisecond at a distance of 4,000 yards. People may be injured by flash burns at even larger distances. Gamma radiation danger does not extend nearly so far and neutron radiation danger is still more limited.

The high skin temperatures result from the first flash of high intensity radiation and are probably as significant for injuries as the total dosages which come mainly from the second more sustained burst of radiation. The combination of skin temperature increase plus large ultra-violet flux inside 4,000 yards is injurious in all cases to exposed personnel. Beyond this point there may be cases of injury, depending upon the individual sensitivity. The infra-red dosage is probably less important because of its smaller intensity.

CHARACTERISTICS OF THE DAMAGE CAUSED BY THE ATOMIC BOMBS

The damage to man-made structures caused by the bombs was due to two distinct causes: first the blast, or pressure wave, emanating from the center of the explosion, and, second, the fires which were caused either by the heat of the explosion itself or by the collapse of buildings containing stoves, electrical fixtures, or any other equipment which might produce what is known as a secondary fire, and subsequent spread of these fires.

The blast produced by the atomic bomb has already been stated to be approximately equivalent to that of 20,000 tons of T.N.T. Given this figure, one may calculate the expected peak pressures in the air, at various distances from the center of the explosion, which occurred following detonation of the bomb. The peak pressures which were calculated before the bombs were dropped agreed very closely with those which were actually experienced in the cities during the attack as computed by Allied experts in a number of ingenious ways after the occupation of Japan.

The blast of pressure from the atomic bombs differed from that of ordinary high explosive bombs in three main ways:

A. Downward thrust. Because the explosions were well up in the air, much of the damage resulted from a downward pressure. This pressure of course most largely effected flat roofs. Some telegraph and other poles immediately below the explosion remained upright while those at greater distances from the center of damage, being more largely exposed to a horizontal thrust from the blast pressure waves, were overturned or tilted. Trees underneath the explosion remained upright but had their branches broken downward.

B. Mass distortion of buildings. An ordinary bomb can damage only a part of a large building, which may then collapse further under the action of gravity. But the blast wave from an atomic bomb is so large that it can engulf whole buildings, no matter how great their size, pushing them over as though a giant hand had given them a shove.

C. Long duration of the positive pressure pulse and consequent small effect of the negative pressure, or suction, phase. In any explosion, the positive pressure exerted by the blast lasts for a definite period of time (usually a small fraction of a second) and is then followed by a somewhat longer period of negative pressure, or suction. The negative pressure is always much weaker than the positive, but in ordinary explosions the short duration of the positive pulse results in many structures not having time to fail in that phase, while they are able to fail under the more extended, though weaker, negative pressure. But the duration of the positive pulse is approximately proportional to the 1/3 power of the size of the explosive charge. Thus, if the relation held true throughout the range in question, a 10-ton T.N.T. explosion would have a positive pulse only about 1/14th as long as that of a 20,000-ton explosion. Consequently, the atomic explosions had positive pulses so much longer then those of ordinary explosives that nearly all failures probably occurred during this phase, and very little damage could be attributed to the suction which followed.

One other interesting feature was the combination of flash ignition and comparative slow pressure wave. Some objects, such as thin, dry wooden slats, were ignited by the radiated flash heat, and then their fires were blown out some time later (depending on their distance from X) by the pressure blast which followed the flash radiation.

CALCULATIONS OF THE PEAK PRESSURE OF THE BLAST WAVE

Several ingenious methods were used by the various investigators to determine, upon visiting the wrecked cities, what had actually been the peak pressures exerted by the atomic blasts. These pressures were computed for various distances from X, and curves were then plotted which were checked against the theoretical predictions of what the pressures would be. A further check was afforded from the readings obtained by the measuring instruments which were dropped by parachute at each atomic attack. The peak pressure figures gave a direct clue to the equivalent T.N.T. tonnage of the atomic bombs, since the pressures developed by any given amount of T.N.T. can be calculated easily.

One of the simplest methods of estimating the peak pressure is from crushing of oil drums, gasoline cans, or any other empty thin metal vessel with a small opening. The assumption made is that the blast wave pressure comes on instantaneously, the resulting pressure on the can is more than the case can withstand, and the walls collapse inward. The air inside is compressed adiabatically to such a point that the pressure inside is less by a certain amount than the pressure outside, this amount being the pressure difference outside and in that the walls can stand in their crumpled condition. The uncertainties involved are, first, that some air rushes in through any opening that the can may have, and thus helps to build up the pressure inside; and, second, that as the pressure outside falls, the air inside cannot escape sufficiently fast to avoid the walls of the can being blown out again to some extent. These uncertainties are such that estimates of pressure based on this method are on the low side, i.e., they are underestimated.

Another method of calculating the peak-pressure is through the bending of steel flagpoles, or lightning conductors, away from the explosion. It is possible to calculate the drag on a pole or rod in an airstream of a certain density and velocity; by connecting this drag with the strength of the pole in question, a determination of the pressure wave may be obtained.

Still another method of estimating the peak pressure is through the overturning of memorial stones, of which there are a great quantity in Japan. The dimensions of the stones can be used along with known data on the pressure exerted by wind against flat surfaces, to calculate the desired figure.

LONG RANGE BLAST DAMAGE

There was no consistency in the long range blast damage. Observers often thought that they had found the limit, and then 2,000 feet farther away would find further evidence of damage.

The most impressive long range damage was the collapse of some of the barracks sheds at Kamigo, 23,000 feet south of X in Nagasaki. It was remarkable to see some of the buildings intact to the last details, including the roof and even the windows, and yet next to them a similar building collapsed to ground level.

The limiting radius for severe displacement of roof tiles in Nagasaki was about 10,000 feet although isolated cases were found up to 16,000 feet. In Hiroshima the general limiting radius was about 8,000 feet; however, even at a distance of 26,000 feet from X in Hiroshima, some tiles were displaced.

At Mogi, 7 miles from X in Nagasaki, over steep hills over 600 feet high, about 10% of the glass came out. In nearer, sequestered localities only 4 miles from X, no damage of any kind was caused. An interesting effect was noted at Mogi; eyewitnesses said that they thought a raid was being made on the place; one big flash was seen, then a loud roar, followed at several second intervals by half a dozen other loud reports, from all directions. These successive reports were obviously reflections from the hills surrounding Mogi.

GROUND SHOCK

The ground shock in most cities was very light. Water pipes still carried water and where leaks were visible they were mainly above ground. Virtually all of the damage to underground utilities was caused by the collapse of buildings rather than by any direct exertion of the blast pressure. This fact of course resulted from the bombs' having been exploded high in the air.

SHIELDING, OR SCREENING FROM BLAST

In any explosion, a certain amount of protection from blast may be gained by having any large and substantial object between the protected object and the center of the explosion. This shielding effect was noticeable in the atomic explosions, just as in ordinary cases, although the magnitude of the explosions and the fact that they occurred at a considerable height in the air caused marked differences from the shielding which would have characterized ordinary bomb explosions.

The outstanding example of shielding was that afforded by the hills in the city of Nagasaki; it was the shielding of these hills which resulted in the smaller area of devastation in Nagasaki despite the fact that the bomb used there was not less powerful. The hills gave effective shielding only at such distances from the center of explosion that the blast pressure was becoming critical - that is, was only barely sufficient to cause collapse - for the structure. Houses built in ravines in Nagasaki pointing well away from the center of the explosion survived without damage, but others at similar distances in ravines pointing toward the center of explosion were greatly damaged. In the north of Nagasaki there was a small hamlet about 8,000 feet from the center of explosion; one could see a distinctive variation in the intensity of damage across the hamlet, corresponding with the shadows thrown by a sharp hill.

The best example of shielding by a hill was southeast of the center of explosion in Nagasaki. The damage at 8,000 feet from X consisted of light plaster damage and destruction of about half the windows. These buildings were of European type and were on the reverse side of a steep hill. At the same distance to the south-southeast the damage was considerably greater, i.e., all windows and frames, doors, were damaged and heavy plaster damage and cracks in the brick work also appeared. The contrast may be illustrated also by the fact that at the Nagasaki Prefectural office at 10,800 feet the damage was bad enough for the building to be evacuated, while at the Nagasaki Normal School to which the Prefectural office had been moved, at the same distance, the damage was comparatively light.

Because of the height of the bursts no evidence was expected of the shielding of one building by another, at least up to a considerable radius. It was in fact difficult to find any evidence at any distance of such shielding. There appeared to have been a little shielding of the building behind the Administration Building of the Torpedo Works in Nagasaki, but the benefits were very slight. There was also some evidence that the group of buildings comprising the Medical School in Nagasaki did afford each other mutual protection. On the whole, however, shielding of one building by another was not noticeable.

There was one other peculiar type of shielding, best exhibited by the workers' houses to the north of the torpedo plant in Nagasaki. These were 6,000 to 7,000 feet north of X. The damage to these houses was not nearly as bad as those over a thousand feet farther away from the center of explosion. It seemed as though the great destruction caused in the torpedo plant had weakened the blast a little, and the full power was not restored for another 1,000 feet or more.

FLASH BURN

As already stated, a characteristic feature of the atomic bomb, which is quite foreign to ordinary explosives, is that a very appreciable fraction of the energy liberated goes into radiant heat and light. For a sufficiently large explosion, the flash burn produced by this radiated energy will become the dominant cause of damage, since the area of burn damage will increase in proportion to the energy released, whereas the area of blast damage increases only with the two-thirds power of the energy. Although such a reversal of the mechanism of damage was not achieved in the Hiroshima and Nagasaki bombs, the effects of the flash were, however, very evident, and many casualties resulted from flash burns. A discussion of the casualties caused by flash burns will be given later; in this section will be described the other flash effects which were observed in the two cities.

The duration of the heat radiation from the bomb is so short, just a few thousandths of a second, that there is no time for the energy falling on a surface to be dissipated by thermal defusion; the flash burn is typically a surface effect. In other words the surface of either a person or an object exposed to the flash is raised to a very high temperature while immediately beneath the surface very little rise in temperature occurs.

The flash burning of the surface of objects, particularly wooden objects, occurred in Hiroshima up to a radius of 9,500 feet from X; at Nagasaki burns were visible up to 11,000 feet from X. The charring and blackening of all telephone poles, trees and wooden posts in the areas not destroyed by the general fire occurred only on the side facing the center of explosion and did not go around the corners of buildings or hills. The exact position of the explosion was in fact accurately determined by taking a number of sights from various objects which had been flash burned on one side only.

To illustrate the effects of the flash burn, the following describes a number of examples found by an observer moving northward from the center of explosion in Nagasaki. First occurred a row of fence posts at the north edge of the prison hill, at 0.3 miles from X. The top and upper part of these posts were heavily charred. The charring on the front of the posts was sharply limited by the shadow of a wall. This wall had however been completely demolished by the blast, which of course arrived some time after the flash. At the north edge of the Torpedo works, 1.05 miles from X, telephone poles were charred to a depth of about 0.5 millimeters. A light piece of wood similar to the flat side of an orange crate, was found leaning against one of the telephone poles. Its front surface was charred the same way as the pole, but it was evident that it had actually been ignited. The wood was blackened through a couple of cracks and nail holes, and around the edges onto the back surface. It seemed likely that this piece of wood had flamed up under the flash for a few seconds before the flame was blown out by the wind of the blast. Farther out, between 1.05 and 1.5 miles from the explosion, were many trees and poles showing a blackening. Some of the poles had platforms near the top. The shadows cast by the platforms were clearly visible and showed that the bomb had detonated at a considerable height. The row of poles turned north and crossed the mountain ridge; the flash burn was plainly visible all the way to the top of the ridge, the farthest burn observed being at 2.0 miles from X.

Another striking effect of the flash burn was the autumnal appearance of the bowl formed by the hills on three sides of the explosion point. The ridges are about 1.5 miles from X. Throughout this bowl the foliage turned yellow, although on the far side of the ridges the countryside was quite green. This autumnal appearance of the trees extended to about 8,000 feet from X.

However, shrubs and small plants quite near the center of explosion in Hiroshima, although stripped of leaves, had obviously not been killed. Many were throwing out new buds when observers visited the city.

There are two other remarkable effects of the heat radiated from the bomb explosion. The first of these is the manner in which heat roughened the surface of polished granite, which retained its polish only where it was shielded from the radiated heat travelling in straight lines from the explosion. This roughening by radiated heat caused by the unequal expansion of the constituent crystals of the stone; for granite crystals the melting temperature is about 600 deg centigrade. Therefore the depth of roughening and ultimate flaking of the granite surface indicated the depth to which this temperature occurred and helped to determine the average ground temperatures in the instant following the explosion. This effect was noted for distances about 1 1/2 times as great in Nagasaki as in Hiroshima.

The second remarkable effect was the bubbling of roof tile. The size of the bubbles and their extent was proportional to their nearness to the center of explosion and also depended on how squarely the tile itself was faced toward the explosion. The distance ratio of this effect between Nagasaki and Hiroshima was about the same as for the flaking of polished granite.

Various other effects of the radiated heat were noted, including the lightening of asphalt road surfaces in spots which had not been protected from the radiated heat by any object such as that of a person walking along the road. Various other surfaces were discolored in different ways by the radiated heat.

As has already been mentioned the fact that radiant heat traveled only in straight lines from the center

of explosion enabled observers to determine the
direction toward the center of explosion from a
number of different points, by observing the
"shadows" which were cast by intervening objects
where they shielded the otherwise exposed surface
of some object. Thus the center of explosion was
located with considerable accuracy. In a number of
cases these "shadows" also gave an indication of the
height of burst of the bomb and occasionally a
distinct penumbra was found which enabled
observers to calculate the diameter of the ball of fire
at the instant it was exerting the maximum charring
or burning effect.

One more interesting feature connected with heat
radiation was the charring of fabric to different
degrees depending upon the color of the fabric. A
number of instances were recorded in which
persons wearing clothing of various colors received
burns greatly varying in degree, the degree of burn
depending upon the color of the fabric over the skin
in question. For example a shirt of alternate light
and dark gray stripes, each about 1/8 of an inch
wide, had the dark stripes completely burned out
but the light stripes were undamaged; and a piece of
Japanese paper exposed nearly 1 1/2 miles from X
had the characters which were written in black ink
neatly burned out.

CHARACTERISTICS OF THE INJURIES TO PERSONS

Injuries to persons resulting from the atomic

explosions were of the following types:

A. Burns, from 1. Flash radiation of heat 2. Fires started by the explosions. B. Mechanical injuries from collapse of buildings, flying debris, etc. C. Direct effects of the high blast pressure, i.e., straight compression. D. Radiation injuries, from the instantaneous emission of gamma rays and neutrons.

It is impossible to assign exact percentages of casualties to each of the types of injury, because so many victims were injured by more than one effect of the explosions. However, it is certain that the greater part of the casualties resulted from burns and mechanical injures. Col. Warren, one of America's foremost radioligists, stated it is probable that 7 per cent or less of the deaths resulted primarily from radiation disease.

The greatest single factor influencing the occurrence of casualties was the distance of the person concerned from the center of explosion.

Estimates based on the study of a selected group of 900 patients indicated that total casualties occurred as far out as 14,000 feet at Nagasaki and 12,000 feet at Hiroshima.

Burns were suffered at a considerable greater distance from X than any other type of injury, and mechanical injuries farther out than radiation effects.

Medical findings show that no person was injured

by radioactivity who was not exposed to the actual explosion of the bombs. No injuries resulted from persistent radioactivity of any sort.

BURNS

Two types of burns were observed. These are generally differentiated as flame or fire burn and so-called flash burn.

The early appearance of the flame burn as reported by the Japanese, and the later appearance as observed, was not unusual.

The flash burn presented several distinctive features. Marked redness of the affected skin areas appeared almost immediately, according to the Japanese, with progressive changes in the skin taking place over a period of a few hours. When seen after 50 days, the most distinctive feature of these burns was their sharp limitation to exposed skin areas facing the center of the explosion. For instance, a patient who had been walking in a direction at right angles to a line drawn between him and the explosion, and whose arms were swinging, might have burns only on the outside of the arm nearest the center and on the inside of the other arm.

Generally, any type of shielding protected the skin against flash burns, although burns through one, and very occasionally more, layers of clothing did occur in patients near the center. In such cases, it was not unusual to find burns through black but not through white clothing, on the same patient. Flash burns also tended to involve areas where the clothes were tightly drawn over the skin, such as at the elbows and shoulders.

The Japanese report the incidence of burns in patients surviving more than a few hours after the explosion, and seeking medical attention, as high as 95%. The total mortalities due to burns alone cannot be estimated with any degree of accuracy. As mentioned already, it is believed that the majority of all the deaths occurred immediately. Of these, the Japanese estimate that 75%, and most of the reports estimate that over 50%, of the deaths were due to burns.

In general, the incidence of burns was in direct proportion to the distance from X. However, certain irregularities in this relationship result in the medical studies because of variations in the amount of shielding from flash burn, and because of the lack of complete data on persons killed outright close to X.

The maximum distance from X at which flash burns were observed is of paramount interest. It has been estimated that patients with burns at Hiroshima were all less than 7,500 feet from the center of the explosion at the time of the bombing. At Nagasaki, patients with burns were observed out to the remarkable distance of 13,800 feet.

MECHANICAL INJURIES

The mechanical injuries included fractures, lacerations, contusions, abrasions, and other effects to be expected from falling roofs, crumbling walls, flying debris and glass, and other indirect blast effects. The appearance of these various types of mechanical injuries was not remarkable to the medical authorities who studied them.

It was estimated that patients with lacerations at Hiroshima were less than 10,600 feet from X, whereas at Nagasaki they extended as far as 12,200 feet.

The tremendous drag of wind, even as far as 1 mile from X, must have resulted in many injuries and deaths. Some large pieces of a prison wall, for example, were flung 80 feet, and many have gone 30 feet high before falling. The same fate must have befallen many persons, and the chances of a human being surviving such treatment are probably small.

BLAST INJURIES

No estimate of the number of deaths or early symptoms due to blast pressure can be made. The pressures developed on the ground under the explosions were not sufficient to kill more than those people very near the center of damage (within a few hundred feet at most). Very few cases of ruptured ear drums were noted, and it is the general feeling of the medical authorities that the direct blast effects were not great. Many of the Japanese reports, which are believed to be false, describe immediate effects such as ruptured abdomens with protruding intestines and protruding eyes, but no such results were actually traced to the effect of air pressure alone.

RADIATION INJURIES

As pointed out in another section of this report the radiations from the nuclear explosions which caused injuries to persons were primarily those experienced within the first second after the explosion; a few may have occurred later, but all occurred in the first minute. The other two general types of radiation, viz., radiation from scattered fission products and induced radioactivity from objects near the center of explosion, were definitely proved not to have caused any casualties.

The proper designation of radiation injuries is somewhat difficult. Probably the two most direct designations are radiation injury and gamma ray injury. The former term is not entirely suitable in that it does not define the type of radiation as ionizing and allows possible confusion with other types of radiation (e.g., infra-red). The objection to the latter term is that it limits the ionizing radiation to gamma rays, which were undoubtedly the most important; but the possible contribution of neutron and even beta rays to the biological effects cannot be entirely ignored. Radiation injury has the advantage of custom, since it is generally understood in medicine to refer to X-ray effect as distinguished from the effects of actinic radiation. Accordingly, radiation injury is used in this report to mean injury due only to ionizing radiation.

According to Japanese observations, the early symptons in patients suffering from radiation injury closely resembled the symptons observed in patients receiving intensive roentgen therapy, as well as those observed in experimental animals receiving large doses of X-rays. The important symptoms reported by the Japanese and observed by American authorities were epilation (lose of hair), petechiae (bleeding into the skin), and other hemorrhagic manifestations, oropharyngeal lesions (inflammation of the mouth and throat), vomiting, diarrhea, and fever.

Epilation was one of the most spectacular and obvious findings. The appearance of the epilated patient was typical. The crown was involved more than the sides, and in many instances the resemblance to a monk's tonsure was striking. In extreme cases the hair was totally lost. In some cases, re-growth of hair had begun by the time patients were seen 50 days after the bombing. Curiously, epilation of hair other than that of the scalp was extremely unusual.

Petechiae and other hemorrhagic manifestations were striking findings. Bleeding began usually from the gums and in the more seriously affected was soon evident from every possible source. Petechiae appeared on the limbs and on pressure points. Large ecchymoses (hemorrhages under the skin) developed about needle punctures, and wounds partially healed broke down and bled freely. Retinal hemorrhages occurred in many of the patients. The bleeding time and the coagulation time were prolonged. The platelets (coagulation of the blood) were characteristically reduced in numbers.

Nausea and vomiting appearing within a few hours after the explosion was reported frequently by the Japanese. This usually had subsided by the following morning, although occasionally it continued for two or three days. Vomiting was not infrequently reported and observed during the course of the later symptoms, although at these times it generally appeared to be related to other manifestation of systemic reactions associated with infection.

Diarrhea of varying degrees of severity was reported and observed. In the more severe cases, it was frequently bloody. For reasons which are not yet clear, the diarrhea in some cases was very persistent.

Lesions of the gums, and the oral mucous membrane, and the throat were observed. The affected areas became deep red, then violacious in color; and in many instances ulcerations and necrosis (breakdown of tissue) followed. Blood counts done and recorded by the Japanese, as well as counts done by the Manhattan Engineer District Group, on such patients regularly showed leucopenia (low-white blood cell count). In extreme cases the white blood cell count was below 1,000 (normal count is around 7,000). In association with the leucopenia and the oropharyngeal lesions, a variety of other infective processes were seen. Wounds and burns which were healing adequately suppurated and serious necrosis occurred. At the same time, similar ulcerations were observed in the larynx, bowels, and in females, the gentalia. Fever usually accompanied these lesions.

Eye injuries produced by the atomic bombings in both cities were the subject of special investigations. The usual types of mechanical injuries were seen. In addition, lesions consisting of retinal hemorrhage and exudation were observed and 75% of the patients showing them had other signs of radiation injury.

The progress of radiation disease of various degrees of severity is shown in the following table:

Summary of Radiation Injury Clinical Symptoms and Findings

Day after Explo- sion Most Severe Moderately Severe Mild 1. 1. Nausea and vomiting 1. Nausea and vomiting 2. after 1-2 hours. after 1-2 hours. 3. NO DEFINITE SYMPTOMS 4. 5. 2. Diarrhea 6. 3. Vomiting NO DEFINITE SYMPTOMS 7. 4. Inflammation of the mouth and throat 8. 5. Fever 9. 6. Rapid emaciation 10. Death NO DEFINITE SYMPTOMS 11. (Mortality probably 2. Beginning epilation. 12. 100%) 13. 14. 15. 16. 17. 18. 3. Loss of appetite 19. and general malaise. 1. Epilation 20. 4. Fever. 2. Loss of appetite 21. 5. Severe inflammation and malaise. 22. of the mouth and throat 3. Sore throat. 23. 4. Pallor. 24. 5. Petechiae

25. 6. Diarrhea 26. 7. Moderate emacia- 27. 6.
Pallor. tion. 28. 7. Petechiae, diarrhea 29. and nose
bleeds (Recovery unless com- 30. plicated by
previous 31. 8. Rapid emaciation poor health or
Death super-imposed in- (Mortality probably 50%)
juries or infec- tion).

It was concluded that persons exposed to the bombs
at the time of detonation did show effects from
ionizing radiation and that some of these patients,
otherwise uninjured, died. Deaths from radiation
began about a week after exposure and reached a
peak in 3 to 4 weeks. They practically ceased to
occur after 7 to 8 weeks.

Treatment of the burns and other physical injuries
was carried out by the Japanese by orthodox
methods. Treatment of radiation effects by them
included general supportative measures such as rest
and high vitamin and caloric diets. Liver and
calcium preparations were administered by injection
and blood transfusions were used to combat
hemorrhage. Special vitamin preparations and other
special drugs used in the treatment of similar
medical conditions were used by American Army
Medical Corps officers after their arrival. Although
the general measures instituted were of some
benefit no definite effect of any of the specific
measures on the course of the disease could be
demonstrated. The use of sulfonamide drugs by the
Japanese and particularly of penicillin by the
American physicians after their arrival undoubtedly
helped control the infections and they appear to be
the single important type of treatment which may
have effectively altered the earlier course of these

patients.

One of the most important tasks assigned to the mission which investigated the effects of the bombing was that of determining if the radiation effects were all due to the instantaneous discharges at the time of the explosion, or if people were being harmed in addition from persistent radioactivity. This question was investigated from two points of view. Direct measurements of persistent radioactivity were made at the time of the investigation. From these measurements, calculations were made of the graded radiation dosages, i.e., the total amount of radiation which could have been absorbed by any person. These calculations showed that the highest dosage which would have been received from persistent radioactivity at Hiroshima was between 6 and 25 roentgens of gamma radiation; the highest in the Nagasaki Area was between 30 and 110 roentgens of gamma radiation. The latter figure does not refer to the city itself, but to a localized area in the Nishiyama District. In interpreting these findings it must be understood that to get these dosages, one would have had to remain at the point of highest radioactivity for 6 weeks continuously, from the first hour after the bombing. It is apparent therefore that insofar as could be determined at Hiroshima and Nagasaki, the residual radiation alone could not have been detrimental to the health of persons entering and living in the bombed areas after the explosion.

The second approach to this question was to determine if any persons not in the city at the time of the explosion, but coming in immediately afterwards exhibited any symptoms or findings which might have been due to persistence induced radioactivity. By the time of the arrival of the Manhattan Engineer District group, several Japanese studies had been done on such persons. None of the persons examined in any of these studies showed any symptoms which could be attributed to radiation, and their actual blood cell counts were consistently within the normal range. Throughout the period of the Manhattan Engineer District investigation, Japanese doctors and patients were repeatedly requested to bring to them any patients who they thought might be examples of persons harmed from persistent radioactivity. No such subjects were found.

It was concluded therefore as a result of these findings and lack of findings, that although a measurable quantity of induced radioactivity was found, it had not been sufficient to cause any harm to persons living in the two cities after the bombings.

SHIELDING FROM RADIATION

Exact figures on the thicknesses of various substances to provide complete or partial protection from the effects of radiation in relation to the distance from the center of explosion, cannot be released at this time. Studies of collected data are still under way. It can be stated, however, that at a reasonable distance, say about 1/2 mile from the center of explosion, protection to persons from radiation injury can be afforded by a layer of concrete or other material whose thickness does not preclude reasonable construction.

Radiation ultimately caused the death of the few persons not killed by other effects and who were fully exposed to the bombs up to a distance of about 1/2 mile from X. The British Mission has estimated that people in the open had a 50% chance of surviving the effects of radiation at 3/4 of a mile from X.

EFFECTS OF THE ATOMIC BOMBINGS ON THE INHABITANTS OF THE BOMBED CITIES

In both Hiroshima and Nagasaki the tremendous scale of the disaster largely destroyed the cities as entities. Even the worst of all other previous bombing attacks on Germany and Japan, such as the incendiary raids on Hamburg in 1943 and on Tokyo in 1945, were not comparable to the paralyzing effect of the atomic bombs. In addition to the huge number of persons who were killed or injuried so that their services in rehabilitation were not available, a panic flight of the population took place from both cities immediately following the atomic explosions. No significant reconstruction or repair work was accomplished because of the slow return of the population; at the end of November 1945 each of the cities had only about 140,000 people. Although the ending of the war almost immediately after the atomic bombings removed much of the incentive of the Japanese people toward immediate reconstruction of their losses, their paralysis was still remarkable. Even the clearance of wreckage and the burning of the many bodies trapped in it were not well organized some weeks after the bombings. As the British Mission has stated, "the impression which both cities make is of having sunk, in an instant and without a struggle, to the most primitive level."

Aside from physical injury and damage, the most significant effect of the atomic bombs was the sheer terror which it struck into the peoples of the bombed cities. This terror, resulting in immediate hysterical activity and flight from the cities, had one especially pronounced effect: persons who had become accustomed to mass air raids had grown to pay little heed to single planes or small groups of planes, but after the atomic bombings the appearance of a single plane caused more terror and disruption of normal life than the appearance of many hundreds of planes had ever been able to cause before. The effect of this terrible fear of the potential danger from even a single enemy plane on the lives of the peoples of the world in the event of any future war can easily be conjectured.

The atomic bomb did not alone win the war against Japan, but it most certainly ended it, saving the thousands of Allied lives that would have been lost in any combat invasion of Japan.

EYEWITNESS ACCOUNT Hiroshima -- August

6th, 1945

by Father John A. Siemes, professor of modern
philosphy at Tokyo's Catholic University

Up to August 6th, occasional bombs, which did no
great damage, had fallen on Hiroshima. Many cities
roundabout, one after the other, were destroyed, but
Hiroshima itself remained protected. There were
almost daily observation planes over the city but
none of them dropped a bomb. The citizens
wondered why they alone had remained undisturbed
for so long a time. There were fantastic rumors that
the enemy had something special in mind for this
city, but no one dreamed that the end would come
in such a fashion as on the morning of August 6th.

August 6th began in a bright, clear, summer
morning. About seven o'clock, there was an air raid
alarm which we had heard almost every day and a
few planes appeared over the city. No one paid any
attention and at about eight o'clock, the all-clear
was sounded. I am sitting in my room at the
Novitiate of the Society of Jesus in Nagatsuke;
during the past half year, the philosophical and
theological section of our Mission had been
evacuated to this place from Tokyo. The Novitiate
is situated approximately two kilometers from
Hiroshima, half-way up the sides of a broad valley
which stretches from the town at sea level into this
mountainous hinterland, and through which courses
a river. From my window, I have a wonderful view
down the valley to the edge of the city.

Suddenly--the time is approximately 8:14--the

whole valley is filled by a garish light which
resembles the magnesium light used in
photography, and I am conscious of a wave of heat.
I jump to the window to find out the cause of this
remarkable phenomenon, but I see nothing more
than that brilliant yellow light. As I make for the
door, it doesn't occur to me that the light might have
something to do with enemy planes. On the way
from the window, I hear a moderately loud
explosion which seems to come from a distance
and, at the same time, the windows are broken in
with a loud crash. There has been an interval of
perhaps ten seconds since the flash of light. I am
sprayed by fragments of glass. The entire window
frame has been forced into the room. I realize now
that a bomb has burst and I am under the impression
that it exploded directly over our house or in the
immediate vicinity.

I am bleeding from cuts about the hands and head. I
attempt to get out of the door. It has been forced
outwards by the air pressure and has become
jammed. I force an opening in the door by means of
repeated blows with my hands and feet and come to
a broad hallway from which open the various
rooms. Everything is in a state of confusion. All
windows are broken and all the doors are forced
inwards. The bookshelves in the hallway have
tumbled down. I do not note a second explosion and
the fliers seem to have gone on. Most of my
colleagues have been injured by fragments of glass.
A few are bleeding but none has been seriously
injured. All of us have been fortunate since it is now
apparent that the wall of my room opposite the
window has been lacerated by long fragments of

glass.

We proceed to the front of the house to see where the bomb has landed. There is no evidence, however, of a bomb crater; but the southeast section of the house is very severely damaged. Not a door nor a window remains. The blast of air had penetrated the entire house from the southeast, but the house still stands. It is constructed in a Japanese style with a wooden framework, but has been greatly strengthened by the labor of our Brother Gropper as is frequently done in Japanese homes. Only along the front of the chapel which adjoins the house, three supports have given way (it has been made in the manner of Japanese temple, entirely out of wood.)

Down in the valley, perhaps one kilometer toward the city from us, several peasant homes are on fire and the woods on the opposite side of the valley are aflame. A few of us go over to help control the flames. While we are attempting to put things in order, a storm comes up and it begins to rain. Over the city, clouds of smoke are rising and I hear a few slight explosions. I come to the conclusion that an incendiary bomb with an especially strong explosive action has gone off down in the valley. A few of us saw three planes at great altitude over the city at the time of the explosion. I, myself, saw no aircraft whatsoever.

Perhaps a half-hour after the explosion, a procession of people begins to stream up the valley from the city. The crowd thickens continuously. A few come up the road to our house. We give them first aid and bring them into the chapel, which we have in the meantime cleaned and cleared of wreckage, and put them to rest on the straw mats which constitute the floor of Japanese houses. A few display horrible wounds of the extremities and back. The small quantity of fat which we possessed during this time of war was soon used up in the care of the burns. Father Rektor who, before taking holy orders, had studied medicine, ministers to the injured, but our bandages and drugs are soon gone. We must be content with cleansing the wounds.

More and more of the injured come to us. The least injured drag the more seriously wounded. There are wounded soldiers, and mothers carrying burned children in their arms. From the houses of the farmers in the valley comes word: "Our houses are full of wounded and dying. Can you help, at least by taking the worst cases?" The wounded come from the sections at the edge of the city. They saw the bright light, their houses collapsed and buried the inmates in their rooms. Those that were in the open suffered instantaneous burns, particularly on the lightly clothed or unclothed parts of the body. Numerous fires sprang up which soon consumed the entire district. We now conclude that the epicenter of the explosion was at the edge of the city near the Jokogawa Station, three kilometers away from us. We are concerned about Father Kopp who that same morning, went to hold Mass at the Sisters of the Poor, who have a home for children at the edge of the city. He had not returned as yet.

Toward noon, our large chapel and library are filled with the seriously injured. The procession of refugees from the city continues. Finally, about one o'clock, Father Kopp returns, together with the Sisters. Their house and the entire district where they live has burned to the ground. Father Kopp is bleeding about the head and neck, and he has a large burn on the right palm. He was standing in front of the nunnery ready to go home. All of a sudden, he became aware of the light, felt the wave of heat and a large blister formed on his hand. The windows were torn out by the blast. He thought that the bomb had fallen in his immediate vicinity. The nunnery, also a wooden structure made by our Brother Gropper, still remained but soon it is noted that the house is as good as lost because the fire, which had begun at many points in the neighborhood, sweeps closer and closer, and water is not available. There is still time to rescue certain things from the house and to bury them in an open spot. Then the house is swept by flame, and they fight their way back to us along the shore of the river and through the burning streets.

Soon comes news that the entire city has been destroyed by the explosion and that it is on fire. What became of Father Superior and the three other Fathers who were at the center of the city at the Central Mission and Parish House? We had up to this time not given them a thought because we did not believe that the effects of the bomb encompassed the entire city. Also, we did not want to go into town except under pressure of dire necessity, because we thought that the population was greatly perturbed and that it might take revenge on any foreigners which they might consider spiteful onlookers of their misfortune, or even spies.

Father Stolte and Father Erlinghagen go down to
the road which is still full of refugees and bring in
the seriously injured who have sunken by the
wayside, to the temporary aid station at the village
school. There iodine is applied to the wounds but
they are left uncleansed. Neither ointments nor
other therapeutic agents are available. Those that
have been brought in are laid on the floor and no
one can give them any further care. What could one
do when all means are lacking? Under those
circumstances, it is almost useless to bring them in.
Among the passersby, there are many who are
uninjured. In a purposeless, insensate manner,
distraught by the magnitude of the disaster most of
them rush by and none conceives the thought of
organizing help on his own initiative. They are
concerned only with the welfare of their own
families. It became clear to us during these days
that the Japanese displayed little initiative,
preparedness, and organizational skill in
preparation for catastrophes. They failed to carry
out any rescue work when something could have
been saved by a cooperative effort, and fatalistically
let the catastrophe take its course. When we urged
them to take part in the rescue work, they did
everything willingly, but on their own initiative
they did very little.

At about four o'clock in the afternoon, a theology
student and two kindergarten children, who lived at
the Parish House and adjoining buildings which had
burned down, came in and said that Father Superior
LaSalle and Father Schiffer had been seriously
injured and that they had taken refuge in Asano
Park on the river bank. It is obvious that we must

bring them in since they are too weak to come here on foot.

Hurriedly, we get together two stretchers and seven of us rush toward the city. Father Rektor comes along with food and medicine. The closer we get to the city, the greater is the evidence of destruction and the more difficult it is to make our way. The houses at the edge of the city are all severely damaged. Many have collapsed or burned down. Further in, almost all of the dwellings have been damaged by fire. Where the city stood, there is a gigantic burned-out scar. We make our way along the street on the river bank among the burning and smoking ruins. Twice we are forced into the river itself by the heat and smoke at the level of the street.

Frightfully burned people beckon to us. Along the way, there are many dead and dying. On the Misasi Bridge, which leads into the inner city we are met by a long procession of soldiers who have suffered burns. They drag themselves along with the help of staves or are carried by their less severely injured comrades...an endless procession of the unfortunate.

Abandoned on the bridge, there stand with sunken heads a number of horses with large burns on their flanks. On the far side, the cement structure of the local hospital is the only building that remains standing. Its interior, however, has been burned out. It acts as a landmark to guide us on our way.

Finally we reach the entrance of the park. A large proportion of the populace has taken refuge there, but even the trees of the park are on fire in several places. Paths and bridges are blocked by the trunks of fallen trees and are almost impassable. We are told that a high wind, which may well have resulted from the heat of the burning city, has uprooted the large trees. It is now quite dark. Only the fires, which are still raging in some places at a distance, give out a little light.

At the far corner of the park, on the river bank itself, we at last come upon our colleagues. Father Schiffer is on the ground pale as a ghost. He has a deep incised wound behind the ear and has lost so much blood that we are concerned about his chances for survival. The Father Superior has suffered a deep wound of the lower leg. Father Cieslik and Father Kleinsorge have minor injuries but are completely exhausted.

While they are eating the food that we have brought along, they tell us of their experiences. They were in their rooms at the Parish House--it was a quarter after eight, exactly the time when we had heard the explosion in Nagatsuke--when came the intense light and immediately thereafter the sound of breaking windows, walls and furniture. They were showered with glass splinters and fragments of wreckage. Father Schiffer was buried beneath a portion of a wall and suffered a severe head injury. The Father Superior received most of the splinters in his back and lower extremity from which he bled copiously. Everything was thrown about in the rooms themselves, but the wooden framework of the house remained intact. The solidity of the structure which was the work of Brother Gropper again shone forth.

They had the same impression that we had in Nagatsuke: that the bomb had burst in their immediate vicinity. The Church, school, and all buildings in the immediate vicinity collapsed at once. Beneath the ruins of the school, the children cried for help. They were freed with great effort. Several others were also rescued from the ruins of nearby dwellings. Even the Father Superior and Father Schiffer despite their wounds, rendered aid to others and lost a great deal of blood in the process.

In the meantime, fires which had begun some distance away are raging even closer, so that it becomes obvious that everything would soon burn down. Several objects are rescued from the Parish House and were buried in a clearing in front of the Church, but certain valuables and necessities which had been kept ready in case of fire could not be found on account of the confusion which had been wrought. It is high time to flee, since the oncoming flames leave almost no way open. Fukai, the secretary of the Mission, is completely out of his mind. He does not want to leave the house and explains that he does not want to survive the destruction of his fatherland. He is completely uninjured. Father Kleinsorge drags him out of the house on his back and he is forcefully carried away.

Beneath the wreckage of the houses along the way, many have been trapped and they scream to be rescued from the oncoming flames. They must be left to their fate. The way to the place in the city to

which one desires to flee is no longer open and one
must make for Asano Park. Fukai does not want to
go further and remains behind. He has not been
heard from since. In the park, we take refuge on the
bank of the river. A very violent whirlwind now
begins to uproot large trees, and lifts them high into
the air. As it reaches the water, a waterspout forms
which is approximately 100 meters high. The
violence of the storm luckily passes us by. Some
distance away, however, where numerous refugees
have taken shelter, many are blown into the river.
Almost all who are in the vicinity have been injured
and have lost relatives who have been pinned under
the wreckage or who have been lost sight of during
the flight. There is no help for the wounded and
some die. No one pays any attention to a dead man
lying nearby.

The transportation of our own wounded is difficult.
It is not possible to dress their wounds properly in
the darkness, and they bleed again upon slight
motion. As we carry them on the shaky litters in the
dark over fallen trees of the park, they suffer
unbearable pain as the result of the movement, and
lose dangerously large quantities of blood. Our
rescuing angel in this difficult situation is a
Japanese Protestant pastor. He has brought up a
boat and offers to take our wounded up stream to a
place where progress is easier. First, we lower the
litter containing Father Schiffer into the boat and
two of us accompany him. We plan to bring the
boat back for the Father Superior. The boat returns
about one-half hour later and the pastor requests
that several of us help in the rescue of two children
whom he had seen in the river. We rescue them.

They have severe burns. Soon they suffer chills and die in the park.

The Father Superior is conveyed in the boat in the same manner as Father Schiffer. The theology student and myself accompany him. Father Cieslik considers himself strong enough to make his way on foot to Nagatsuke with the rest of us, but Father Kleinsorge cannot walk so far and we leave him behind and promise to come for him and the housekeeper tomorrow. From the other side of the stream comes the whinny of horses who are threatened by the fire. We land on a sand spit which juts out from the shore. It is full of wounded who have taken refuge there. They scream for aid for they are afraid of drowning as the river may rise with the sea, and cover the sand spit. They themselves are too weak to move. However, we must press on and finally we reach the spot where the group containing Father Schiffer is waiting.

Here a rescue party had brought a large case of fresh rice cakes but there is no one to distribute them to the numerous wounded that lie all about. We distribute them to those that are nearby and also help ourselves. The wounded call for water and we come to the aid of a few. Cries for help are heard from a distance, but we cannot approach the ruins from which they come. A group of soldiers comes along the road and their officer notices that we speak a strange language. He at once draws his sword, screamingly demands who we are and threatens to cut us down. Father Laures, Jr., seizes his arm and explains that we are German. We finally quiet him down. He thought that we might

well be Americans who had parachuted down.
Rumors of parachutists were being bandied about
the city. The Father Superior who was clothed only
in a shirt and trousers, complains of feeling freezing
cold, despite the warm summer night and the heat of
the burning city. The one man among us who
possesses a coat gives it to him and, in addition, I
give him my own shirt. To me, it seems more
comfortable to be without a shirt in the heat.

In the meantime, it has become midnight. Since
there are not enough of us to man both litters with
four strong bearers, we determine to remove Father
Schiffer first to the outskirts of the city. From there,
another group of bearers is to take over to
Nagatsuke; the others are to turn back in order to
rescue the Father Superior. I am one of the bearers.
The theology student goes in front to warn us of the
numerous wires, beams and fragments of ruins
which block the way and which are impossible to
see in the dark. Despite all precautions, our progress
is stumbling and our feet get tangled in the wire.
Father Kruer falls and carries the litter with him.
Father Schiffer becomes half unconscious from the
fall and vomits. We pass an injured man who sits all
alone among the hot ruins and whom I had seen
previously on the way down.

On the Misasa Bridge, we meet Father Tappe and
Father Luhmer, who have come to meet us from
Nagatsuke. They had dug a family out of the ruins
of their collapsed house some fifty meters off the
road. The father of the family was already dead.
They had dragged out two girls and placed them by
the side of the road. Their mother was still trapped

under some beams. They had planned to complete
the rescue and then to press on to meet us. At the
outskirts of the city, we put down the litter and
leave two men to wait until those who are to come
from Nagatsuke appear. The rest of us turn back to
fetch the Father Superior.

Most of the ruins have now burned down. The
darkness kindly hides the many forms that lie on the
ground. Only occasionally in our quick progress do
we hear calls for help. One of us remarks that the
remarkable burned smell reminds him of incinerated
corpses. The upright, squatting form which we had
passed by previously is still there.

Transportation on the litter, which has been
constructed out of boards, must be very painful to
the Father Superior, whose entire back is full of
fragments of glass. In a narrow passage at the edge
of town, a car forces us to the edge of the road. The
litter bearers on the left side fall into a two meter
deep ditch which they could not see in the darkness.
Father Superior hides his pain with a dry joke, but
the litter which is now no longer in one piece
cannot be carried further. We decide to wait until
Kinjo can bring a hand cart from Nagatsuke. He
soon comes back with one that he has requisitioned
from a collapsed house. We place Father Superior
on the cart and wheel him the rest of the way,
avoiding as much as possible the deeper pits in the
road.

About half past four in the morning, we finally
arrive at the Novitiate. Our rescue expedition had
taken almost twelve hours. Normally, one could go

back and forth to the city in two hours. Our two wounded were now, for the first time, properly dressed. I get two hours sleep on the floor; some one else has taken my own bed. Then I read a Mass in gratiarum actionem, it is the 7th of August, the anniversary of the foundation of our society. Then we bestir ourselves to bring Father Kleinsorge and other acquaintances out of the city.

We take off again with the hand cart. The bright day now reveals the frightful picture which last night's darkness had partly concealed. Where the city stood everything, as far as the eye could reach, is a waste of ashes and ruin. Only several skeletons of buildings completely burned out in the interior remain. The banks of the river are covered with dead and wounded, and the rising waters have here and there covered some of the corpses. On the broad street in the Hakushima district, naked burned cadavers are particularly numerous. Among them are the wounded who are still alive. A few have crawled under the burnt-out autos and trams. Frightfully injured forms beckon to us and then collapse. An old woman and a girl whom she is pulling along with her fall down at our feet. We place them on our cart and wheel them to the hospital at whose entrance a dressing station has been set up. Here the wounded lie on the hard floor, row on row. Only the largest wounds are dressed. We convey another soldier and an old woman to the place but we cannot move everybody who lies exposed in the sun. It would be endless and it is questionable whether those whom we can drag to the dressing station can come out alive, because even here nothing really effective can be done.

Later, we ascertain that the wounded lay for days in the burnt-out hallways of the hospital and there they died.

We must proceed to our goal in the park and are forced to leave the wounded to their fate. We make our way to the place where our church stood to dig up those few belongings that we had buried yesterday. We find them intact. Everything else has been completely burned. In the ruins, we find a few molten remnants of holy vessels. At the park, we load the housekeeper and a mother with her two children on the cart. Father Kleinsorge feels strong enough, with the aid of Brother Nobuhara, to make his way home on foot. The way back takes us once again past the dead and wounded in Hakushima. Again no rescue parties are in evidence. At the Misasa Bridge, there still lies the family which the Fathers Tappe and Luhmer had yesterday rescued from the ruins. A piece of tin had been placed over them to shield them from the sun. We cannot take them along for our cart is full. We give them and those nearby water to drink and decide to rescue them later. At three o'clock in the afternoon, we are back in Nagatsuka.

After we have had a few swallows and a little food, Fathers Stolte, Luhmer, Erlinghagen and myself, take off once again to bring in the family. Father Kleinsorge requests that we also rescue two children who had lost their mother and who had lain near him in the park. On the way, we were greeted by strangers who had noted that we were on a mission of mercy and who praised our efforts. We now met groups of individuals who were carrying

the wounded about on litters. As we arrived at the
Misasa Bridge, the family that had been there was
gone. They might well have been borne away in the
meantime. There was a group of soldiers at work
taking away those that had been sacrificed
yesterday.

More than thirty hours had gone by until the first
official rescue party had appeared on the scene. We
find both children and take them out of the park: a
six-year old boy who was uninjured, and a twelve-
year old girl who had been burned about the head,
hands and legs, and who had lain for thirty hours
without care in the park. The left side of her face
and the left eye were completely covered with blood
and pus, so that we thought that she had lost the
eye. When the wound was later washed, we noted
that the eye was intact and that the lids had just
become stuck together. On the way home, we took
another group of three refugees with us. They first
wanted to know, however, of what nationality we
were. They, too, feared that we might be Americans
who had parachuted in. When we arrived in
Nagatsuka, it had just become dark.

We took under our care fifty refugees who had lost
everything. The majority of them were wounded
and not a few had dangerous burns. Father Rektor
treated the wounds as well as he could with the few
medicaments that we could, with effort, gather up.
He had to confine himself in general to cleansing
the wounds of purulent material. Even those with
the smaller burns are very weak and all suffered
from diarrhea. In the farm houses in the vicinity,
almost everywhere, there are also wounded. Father

Rektor made daily rounds and acted in the capacity of a painstaking physician and was a great Samaritan. Our work was, in the eyes of the people, a greater boost for Christianity than all our work during the preceding long years.

Three of the severely burned in our house died within the next few days. Suddenly the pulse and respirations ceased. It is certainly a sign of our good care that so few died. In the official aid stations and hospitals, a good third or half of those that had been brought in died. They lay about there almost without care, and a very high percentage succumbed. Everything was lacking: doctors, assistants, dressings, drugs, etc. In an aid station at a school at a nearby village, a group of soldiers for several days did nothing except to bring in and cremate the dead behind the school.

During the next few days, funeral processions passed our house from morning to night, bringing the deceased to a small valley nearby. There, in six places, the dead were burned. People brought their own wood and themselves did the cremation. Father Luhmer and Father Laures found a dead man in a nearby house who had already become bloated and who emitted a frightful odor. They brought him to this valley and incinerated him themselves. Even late at night, the little valley was lit up by the funeral pyres.

We made systematic efforts to trace our acquaintances and the families of the refugees whom we had sheltered. Frequently, after the passage of several weeks, some one was found in a distant village or hospital but of many there was no news, and these were apparently dead. We were lucky to discover the mother of the two children whom we had found in the park and who had been given up for dead. After three weeks, she saw her children once again. In the great joy of the reunion were mingled the tears for those whom we shall not see again.

The magnitude of the disaster that befell Hiroshima on August 6th was only slowly pieced together in my mind. I lived through the catastrophe and saw it only in flashes, which only gradually were merged to give me a total picture. What actually happened simultaneously in the city as a whole is as follows: As a result of the explosion of the bomb at 8:15, almost the entire city was destroyed at a single blow. Only small outlying districts in the southern and eastern parts of the town escaped complete destruction. The bomb exploded over the center of the city. As a result of the blast, the small Japanese houses in a diameter of five kilometers, which compressed 99% of the city, collapsed or were blown up. Those who were in the houses were buried in the ruins. Those who were in the open sustained burns resulting from contact with the substance or rays emitted by the bomb. Where the substance struck in quantity, fires sprang up. These spread rapidly.

The heat which rose from the center created a whirlwind which was effective in spreading fire throughout the whole city. Those who had been caught beneath the ruins and who could not be freed rapidly, and those who had been caught by the flames, became casualties. As much as six kilometers from the center of the explosion, all houses were damaged and many collapsed and caught fire. Even fifteen kilometers away, windows were broken. It was rumored that the enemy fliers had spread an explosive and incendiary material over the city and then had created the explosion and ignition. A few maintained that they saw the planes drop a parachute which had carried something that exploded at a height of 1,000 meters. The newspapers called the bomb an "atomic bomb" and noted that the force of the blast had resulted from the explosion of uranium atoms, and that gamma rays had been sent out as a result of this, but no one knew anything for certain concerning the nature of the bomb.

How many people were a sacrifice to this bomb? Those who had lived through the catastrophe placed the number of dead at at least 100,000. Hiroshima had a population of 400,000. Official statistics place the number who had died at 70,000 up to September 1st, not counting the missing ... and 130,000 wounded, among them 43,500 severely wounded. Estimates made by ourselves on the basis of groups known to us show that the number of 100,000 dead is not too high. Near us there are two barracks, in each of which forty Korean workers lived. On the day of the explosion, they were laboring on the streets of Hiroshima. Four returned alive to one barracks and sixteen to the other. 600 students of the Protestant girls' school worked in a factory, from which only thirty to forty returned. Most of the peasant families in the neighborhood lost one or more of their members who had worked at factories in the city. Our next door neighbor, Tamura, lost two children and himself suffered a large wound since, as it happened, he had been in the city on that day. The family of our reader suffered two dead, father and son; thus a family of five members suffered at least two losses, counting only the dead and severely wounded. There died the Mayor, the President of the central Japan district, the Commander of the city, a Korean prince who had been stationed in Hiroshima in the capacity of an officer, and many other high ranking officers. Of the professors of the University, thirty-two were killed or severely injured. Especially hard hit were the soldiers. The Pioneer Regiment was almost entirely wiped out. The barracks were near the center of the explosion.

Thousands of wounded who died later could doubtless have been rescued had they received proper treatment and care, but rescue work in a catastrophe of this magnitude had not been envisioned; since the whole city had been knocked out at a blow, everything which had been prepared for emergency work was lost, and no preparation had been made for rescue work in the outlying districts. Many of the wounded also died because they had been weakened by under-nourishment and consequently lacked in strength to recover. Those who had their normal strength and who received good care slowly healed the burns which had been occasioned by the bomb. There were also cases, however, whose prognosis seemed good who died suddenly. There were also some who had only small external wounds who died within a week or later, after an inflammation of the pharynx and oral cavity had taken place. We thought at first that this was the result of inhalation of the substance of the bomb. Later, a commission established the thesis that gamma rays had been given out at the time of the explosion, following which the internal organs had been injured in a manner resembling that consequent upon Roentgen irradiation. This produces a diminution in the numbers of the white corpuscles.

Only several cases are known to me personally where individuals who did not have external burns later died. Father Kleinsorge and Father Cieslik, who were near the center of the explosion, but who did not suffer burns became quite weak some fourteen days after the explosion. Up to this time small incised wounds had healed normally, but thereafter the wounds which were still unhealed became worse and are to date (in September) still incompletely healed. The attending physician diagnosed it as leucopania. There thus seems to be some truth in the statement that the radiation had some effect on the blood. I am of the opinion, however, that their generally undernourished and weakened condition was partly responsible for these findings. It was noised about that the ruins of the city emitted deadly rays and that workers who went there to aid in the clearing died, and that the central district would be uninhabitable for some time to come. I have my doubts as to whether such talk is true and myself and others who worked in the ruined area for some hours shortly after the explosion suffered no such ill effects.

None of us in those days heard a single outburst

against the Americans on the part of the Japanese, nor was there any evidence of a vengeful spirit. The Japanese suffered this terrible blow as part of the fortunes of war ... something to be borne without complaint. During this, war, I have noted relatively little hatred toward the allies on the part of the people themselves, although the press has taken occasion to stir up such feelings. After the victories at the beginning of the war, the enemy was rather looked down upon, but when allied offensive gathered momentum and especially after the advent of the majestic B-29's, the technical skill of America became an object of wonder and admiration.

The following anecdote indicates the spirit of the Japanese: A few days after the atomic bombing, the secretary of the University came to us asserting that the Japanese were ready to destroy San Francisco by means of an equally effective bomb. It is dubious that he himself believed what he told us. He merely wanted to impress upon us foreigners that the Japanese were capable of similar discoveries. In his nationalistic pride, he talked himself into believing this. The Japanese also intimated that the principle of the new bomb was a Japanese discovery. It was only lack of raw materials, they said, which prevented its construction. In the meantime, the Germans were said to have carried the discovery to a further stage and were about to initiate such bombing. The Americans were reputed to have learned the secret from the Germans, and they had then brought the bomb to a stage of industrial completion.

We have discussed among ourselves the ethics of the use of the bomb. Some consider it in the same category as poison gas and were against its use on a civil population. Others were of the view that in total war, as carried on in Japan, there was no difference between civilians and soldiers, and that the bomb itself was an effective force tending to end the bloodshed, warning Japan to surrender and thus to avoid total destruction. It seems logical to me that he who supports total war in principle cannot complain of war against civilians. The crux of the matter is whether total war in its present form is justifiable, even when it serves a just purpose. Does it not have material and spiritual evil as its consequences which far exceed whatever good that might result? When will our moralists give us a clear answer to this question?